Over the Rainbow
The Life and Rhymes of
Yip Harburg

By Stuart Stotts

Over the Rainbow. Copyright 2014 by Stuart Stotts. All rights reserved under the International and Pan-American Copyright Conventions. By payment of the required fees you have been granted the nonexclusive right to access and read the text of this e-book on screen. No part of this text may be reproduced, transmitted, downloaded, decompiled, reverse-engineered, or stored in or introduced into any information storage and retrieval system, in any form or means, whether electronic or mechanical, now known or hereafter invented, without the express written permission of Stuart Stotts, author.

ISBN 9780976537236
Library of Congress Control Number: 2015910442
Stuart Stotts 1957 -

BIG VALLEY PRESS
www.BigValleyPress.com
Big Valley Press supports the First Amendment and celebrates the right to read.

Dedicated to Dr. Richard Dolezal (1935-2012)

A lover of words, poetry, and music

And the greatest teacher I've ever known.

Table of Contents

Foreward

1. Putting in the Rainbow 7
2. A Squirrel on the Lower East Side 10
3. Yip and Gersh: A Lifelong Friendship 17
4. A Business Man Happily Goes Broke 21
5. Learning the Craft 26
6. Brother, Can You Spare a Dime? 29
7. The Hits Keep Coming 34
8. Hollywood 41
9. Off to Write the Wizard 46
10. Over the Rainbow 50
11. Script Doctor 54
12. After the Wizard 57
13. Look to the Rainbow 64
14. Blacklist 71
15. The Sixties 78
16. Legacy 83
17. Lessons from a Lyrical Master 86

Foreward

Yip Harburg was born Isidore Hochberg but wasn't satisfied with the name, so he changed it to Edgar Harburg, eventually going by the nickname Yip. He was raised an Orthodox Jew but wasn't satisfied with that so he spent his adult life as an atheist. He started out dedicated to the career of appliance sales but wasn't satisfied with that so he became a song lyricist. Sometimes he wrote about daydreams as being life's biggest helper ("Follow the fellow that follows the dream") but at other times he wasn't satisfied with that idea and wrote about dreams as being silly ("It's only a paper moon . . . "). Lucky for us, he was not afraid of admitting to being unsatisfied.

Yip's songs demonstrate, as does his life story, that the struggle to find satisfaction is often confusing and difficult. And he makes us feel less alone by showing that this frustrating confusion is common to all humans. No song has ever captured the passionate sorrow of teenage bewilderment and yearning like "Somewhere Over the Rainbow." No song has ever portrayed the desolate disappointment of a society's broken dreams like "Brother Can You Spare a Dime." I am a songwriter myself, and some of what I think are my best songs were consciously influenced by the empathetic writing style of Yip Harburg. Mine aren't as good, of course. Maybe I should change my name and sell toasters for awhile.

Stuart Stotts, a dear friend and award-winning songwriter himself, has exhaustively delved into Yip Harburg's life and work, enthusiastic about spreading the word concerning the man and his methods. I think one of the greatest gifts an artist can give the world is a heightened ability to stand in someone else's shoes. Yip was a genius in this regard, and with this book, Stuart helps us stand for awhile in Yip's shoes.

Peter Berryman, Madison, Wi. December, 2013

Yip as a young man. Beverly Hills, 1930's

CHAPTER 1

Putting in the Rainbow

One of the most popular songs of all time was almost cut from the movie that made it famous. Luckily, its writers kept pushing to include it in *The Wizard of Oz*. Soon, "Over the Rainbow" went on to fame, fortune, and a treasured place in the hearts of millions.

Yip Harburg wrote the lyrics and Harold Arlen composed the music for "Over the Rainbow," a song more commonly called "Somewhere Over the Rainbow." The Recording Industry of America placed it first on its list of top songs of the last 100 years, and the American Film Institute named it the greatest movie song of all time. It's hard to find someone who hasn't heard "Over the Rainbow." And, yet, the song nearly didn't make it into *The Wizard of Oz*.

In 1939, *The Wizard of Oz* was shown in previews in California. Previews, or advance showings, allow a movie's producers to see how audiences react to a new film. If audiences don't like it, a movie can go back to the studio to be changed and, hopefully, improved.

At the end of the first preview, Victor Fleming, one of the film's directors, walked into the movie producer's office and said, "The whole first part of that show is awful slow because of that number 'Over the Rainbow.' We gotta take it out." Others at the movie studio agreed. They believed "Over the Rainbow" wasn't upbeat enough to start the movie. They also thought the music was too grandiose and operatic for a simple farm girl like Dorothy to sing believably.

"Harold and I just went crazy," recalled lyricist Yip. "We knew that this was the ballad of the show . . . We went to the front office, we went to the back office. We pleaded, we cried." The song was restored to the movie, but then cut twice more after two other previews.

Finally, producer Arthur Freed met with the head of the movie studio, Louis B. Mayer, to make his case. Freed threatened to quit if the song wasn't included and Mayer gave in. "Fine," he said. "Let the boys have the damn song. Get it back in the picture; it can't hurt." The song went on to achieve enormous popularity, vindicating the writers in a triumph of artistic intuition. Harold Arlen and Yip Harburg were right all along.

Yip wrote all of the lyrics to the songs in *The Wizard of Oz,* and he played a major role in shaping the overall story. By 1939, he had been creating lyrics for movies and theatrical shows for over ten years. Raised in poverty in New York City, Yip became one of America's greatest and most successful lyricists, writing "It's Only a Paper Moon," "April In Paris," "Brother, Can You Spare a Dime?" and other popular songs. He collaborated with many of the best composers and writers of his time, changing the shape of Broadway shows and movie musicals forever.

Yip knew that songs had power. He didn't just write for entertainment; he wanted to change the world with his songs. He explained why in a lecture. "Magic in song happens only when the words give destination and meaning to the music, and the music gives wings to the words. Together as a song they go places you've never been before. The reason is obvious—words make you think thoughts. Music makes you feel a feeling. But a song makes you feel a thought . . . That's why song is the most powerful weapon there is . . . you can teach more through song and you can rouse more through song than all the prose in the world, or all the poems."

Even when he was blacklisted by his own industry in the 1950s, Yip maintained a positive outlook on living, filled with humor, wit, imagination, and a concern for equality and justice. He didn't quit; he kept on writing right up to the end of his life. His songs remain popular today because they speak to an essential part in all of us, the part inside where dreams really do come true.

Yip and Harold Arlen, California

CHAPTER 2

A Squirrel on the Lower East Side

Yip Harburg was born Isidore Hochberg on April 8, 1896 on the Lower East Side of New York. His parents, Lewis Hochberg and Mary Ricing, arrived from Russia during the tide of immigration in the early 1890s. Yip's parents had ten children, but eight of them died when they were young. Yip himself was a "blue baby," born without color and expected to die. He held on, though, and his life was considered a miracle.

Like most residents of the Lower East Side, Yip's family was poor. His parents worked long hours in a garment factory. Yip remembered his father's gnarled fingers, twisted from work, and how his mother bent over the kitchen sink, washing clothes. His parents were always worried about being evicted for not having enough money to pay the rent.

In the 1890s, the Lower East Side of New York City smelled like pickles, bread, fish, and garbage. Brick and brownstone apartment buildings rose five or six stories overhead, and the sidewalks were crowded with stalls selling food and clothing. Horses tugged wagons through the muddy roads as pushcart vendors sang out advertisements for eggs, shoes, brooms, or dishes. Adults shopped, children ran and played, and Yiddish was the language of the streets. The bustle of traffic and the cries of shopkeepers mixed with music, German bands played in the alleys, and organ grinders cranked out popular songs and bits of opera.

One contemporary writer described the atmosphere. "A gray, stone world of tall tenements, where even on the loveliest spring day there was not a blade of grass . . . the men and women clustered around the pushcarts . . . Buses

and trolleys rushed through the streets with devilish force. Waves of people pounded the streets, their faces like foam . . . It was all wild, all inconceivable."

Beginning in 1881, thousands of Jewish immigrants fled from persecution in Russia and Eastern Europe. Most of them came through Ellis Island or the Castle Garden immigration center and settled in New York. Like other immigrants they came looking for opportunity, but they also came to escape oppression and prejudice. Jews in Europe were often harassed, bloodied, and even killed. They might be driven from their home and land at the whim of a distant ruler or a local lord. America promised freedom to practice their religion and safety for their families. Although children learned English in America, most of their parents spoke Yiddish, a mixture of German and Hebrew.

Yip's parents were among these immigrants. His sister Ann worked fourteen or more hours a day in a shop, and Yip began working when he was just a boy. One of his jobs was lighting and dimming the gaslights along the streets and avenues.

"I'd put the lights on when dusk set in, and then I had to get up at three or four in the morning and go out and turn 'em off!" he said. "I think it was about three miles . . . and it was full of a lot of gangster kids, tough little Irish kids . . . there were the Italian gansters, too, and they were all looking for the little Jewish boy who was lighting lamps. We wore blouses at the time . . . I had my blouses filled up with cigarettes which I picked up . . . butts around the block, distributed them so that I didn't get a bloody nose." For working every morning and night, Yip earned three dollars and sixty cents a week.

Yip didn't have his own room and he didn't even have a bed; he and his sister Anna slept on chairs pushed together. A 1908 survey showed that 3/4 of the families on the Lower East Side slept with at least three people in one room, and many rooms held five or more. People walked up four, five, even six flights of stairs to apartments that often had no heat or toilet, and sometimes not even a window. Everyone shared one thing—poverty.

Later in his life, Yip remembered his impoverished childhood. "You lived from month to month. But youngsters didn't feel the sting of it because everyone else was poor, too. We knew no other way of life and it didn't mean much to a kid who turned the street into an exciting playground."

Growing up poor shaped Yip's outlook. He later quoted famous playwright George Bernard Shaw; he felt "the chill of poverty which never leaves your bones." Yip empathized with his father and his mother's suffering. "I always had hope that someday they would be liberated."

Some people who rise up from poverty merely want to escape their origins. Yip's feelings about poverty reached beyond his parents. He wanted out, but he also wanted for others to be free of poverty and suffering. "I contest anything that is unjust, that causes suffering in humanity," he once said.

This foundation of beliefs about equality and human dignity was central to his lyric writing. His songs show the injustice of the world and allow us to experience the difference between everyday life and our cherished illusions. They also encourage us to endure hardship with laughter.

When Yip was 7, his family moved to a tenement apartment at 649 E. 9th Street, in an area that bordered Italian and Irish neighborhoods. Yip described his life on the streets. "A kid was automatically independent by the time he was eight . . . The street, not your home, was your life . . . Our parents didn't know much about all this . . . Down on the street, you were being Americanized."

Others remembered that time. "The streets were ours. Everyplace else—home, school, shop—belonged to the grownups. We would roam through the city tasting the delights of freedom, discovering possibilities far beyond the reach of our parents." Yip loved being outdoors. He remembered his mother throwing down sandwiches from their fifth floor apartment so he wouldn't have to stop playing and come upstairs.

Ethnic rivalry was common, and street life could be rough. "Among the kids there was plenty of friction," said Yip. "We fought the Italians, we fought the Irish, and both of them fought the Jews." Jews faced prejudice in the city. "You were always conscious of your Jewishness the way a black man is of his blackness," said Yip.

Yip (left) and his brother, Harry. 1904

Yip was athletic, mischievous, and funny, unlike his family, who he described as "frightened people . . . I tried to lift them up with games and fun . . . I moved fast and went from one thing to another and I clowned a lot." His energy and constant movement earned him the nickname of "Yipsl," which means "little squirrel" in a Yiddish dialect. "Yipsl" was later shortened to "Yip."

Yip's family was Orthodox Jewish, and they regularly attended services and practiced the rituals of Judaism. However, Yip's father also loved the theatre. Some weekends he told Yip's mother that they were going to the temple school, but instead he took Yip to see shows.

The shows were in Yiddish, and they were by turns funny, energetic, and deeply tragic. One writer looked back at Yiddish theater. "This was a theatre of vivid trash and raw talent . . . with spectacle . . . high gesture . . . The writers and actors . . . understood that their audiences, seemingly lost in the darkness of the sweatshop, wanted most of all the consolation of glamour."

Yip loved Yiddish theatre, and he began attending vaudeville shows as well, which included many kinds of acts: singers, dancers, comedians, musicians, jugglers, trained animals, acrobats, and more. "Whenever I could rake up a quarter," Yip said, "I would spend weekends in the gallery of the Palace Theatre watching these most wonderful performers: Al Jolson, Fanny Brice . . . Bert Lahr," all of whom were famous entertainers in their day.

Yip loved popular songs. He sang and acted well, and he could recite poems like "Gunga Din" and "The Wreck of the Hesperus" clearly and with emotion. In school, he won prizes for acting and reciting. "I'd read, and there would be twenty-odd kids laughing out loud, and . . . I'd tell myself, 'I want to repeat this experience.'" Schoolteachers encouraged Yip's talents, and one of his teachers even took him to the theater to see *Peter Pan*, where Yip's love for fantasy stories was born.

"As a kid I was always living in a fairy tale world," he said. "It was the easiest way to get out of the slums."

The Lower East Side was full of stories and poetry. Poems and stories helped Jewish immigrants understand their new country and their place in it. One writer commented, "It was hardly an accident that so many people in the 1880s and 90s wrote poems. Every speaker, agitator, journalist, and a great many folk intellectuals turned to poetry."

Yip shared their love. "Basically, I loved the English language, the poetry," he said. "We had inspiring teachers. Those were the beginning, the roots of my passion for rhymes."

The Lower East Side was a highly charged, political environment where family, friends, and neighbors debated current events and argued passionately about business and government policies. Yip's father was a socialist, believing that the government should assist and provide for those in need. Every night Yip's father read the *Jewish Daily Forward*, a socialist newspaper. Socialism seemed like a way to remedy the severe poverty that Yip's family and so many other New York residents faced.

Yip's older brother Max was a brilliant scientist, but he died suddenly at age 26 when Yip was only 14. It was a devastating loss for Yip's whole family, and Yip lost his faith in God as a result. He argued with his father, who continued to believe.

"For you, it's okay," said his father. "You are young. But me, I am an old man. I need insurance."

Yip struggled with questions about religion and belief his whole life, although he most often referred to himself as an atheist. He once said, "I'm trying to find out why I'm alive, why I'm writing songs and why my songs had this commentary of the social system." He wrestled with his questions in poems and songs.

No matter how much I probe and prod

I cannot quite believe in God;

But oh, I hope to God that He

Unswervingly believes in me.

Or

Poems are made by fools like me,

But only God can make a tree;

And only God who makes the tree

Also makes the fools like me.

But only fools like me, you see,

Can make a God, who makes a tree.

Years later Yip was flying to the West Coast with friends. There was engine trouble, and the plane looked like it might crash. One of his friends turned to Yip and said, "Now do you believe in God?"

The plane rocked back and forth. A second engine coughed and sputtered. Yip paused and then replied, "I'll tell you when we land."

Yip spent his childhood on the Lower East Side, immersed in the sounds and smells of the streets. Passionate discussions of politics, history, and religion roiled all around him. Yip's quick mind and good humor took it all in, not yet knowing that one day his lyrics and poems would reflect the richness of his early life.

Yip (right) and his cousin, Lew Corrigan. 1906

CHAPTER 3

Yip and Gersh: A Lifelong Friendship

Yip spent a lot of time as a child trying to keep warm. His apartment had no hot water and only a small coal stove to heat three rooms. If he wanted to be warm while reading or doing his homework, he went to the Tompkins Square Library on Tenth St. where the librarians were delighted to see him.

"There were lovely librarians with blond hair and blue eyes and elegant accents," he remembered. "The attraction was magnetic, and they put me onto some great books . . . My poverty turned into a piece of rather good luck. I mean, otherwise I probably would be doing other things."

Yip loved reading humorous poems and short stories. One of his idols was the writer O. Henry, whom Yip appreciated for the surprising twists that always came at the end of his stories. Yip's biggest literary hero, though, was W.S. Gilbert.

In England in the late 1800's, W.S. Gilbert wrote lyrics for comic operas. His partner, Arthur Sullivan, wrote music for Gilbert's words. Together they created 14 comic operas, including *H.M.S. Pinafore, The Pirates of Penzance, and The Mikado*. Gilbert and Sullivan were wildly popular in the 19th century, and their works are still performed around the world today.

Yip read W.S. Gilbert's verses in the library. He loved the fanciful wordplay and clever rhymes. He also liked how Gilbert used satire to make fun of governments, high society, and pretentious individuals. Yip often used this same satirical approach when he addressed society and its difficulties.

In the opera *Ruddigore* Gilbert argues that you can't advance in society without blowing your own horn, or bragging.

"If you wish in this world to advance,
your merits you're bound to enhance;
You must stir it and stump it,
And blow your own trumpet,
Or trust me, you haven't a chance." (From *Ruddigore*)

In *H.M.S. Pinafore* Gilbert says the safest way to rise in the Navy is to stay safely in the office instead of going to fight on the ocean.

Now landsmen all, whoever you may be,
If you want to rise to the top of the tree.
If your soul isn't fettered to an office stool,
Be careful to be guided by this golden rule -
Stick close to your desks and never go to sea,
And you may all be Rulers of the Queen's Navee." (From *H.M.S. Pinafore*)

When Yip was 16, he attended Townsend Harris School, a preparatory school for City College. Students were seated alphabetically by their last names. A shy boy named Ira Gershwin sat by him—G next to H. One day in class Yip pulled out a book of W.S. Gilbert's poems and began to read. Ira saw the book and became very excited. He leaned over and said to Yip, "Do you know that a lot of this is set to music?" Yip had no idea. He thought that they were just poems. "I'll show you," said Ira.

Ira Gershwin and his brother George later became one of America's most famous songwriting partnerships. They created whole Broadway shows as well, with hits like "I Got Rhythm," "They Can't Take that Away From Me," and "Embraceable You." However, at the time Ira was just a schoolboy who shared Yip's love of poetry. But where Yip was poor, Ira's family was middle class, with enough money to own a Victrola, an old style of record player.

Yip and Ira Gershwin.

Ira invited Yip back to his apartment where they listened to recordings of Gilbert and Sullivan's operas. Yip was astounded to hear the words he had loved on the page being sung to music. "I was thunderstruck, I was flabbergasted," he said later. "I was so delighted . . . I was starry eyed for days. I couldn't sleep at night. It was that music—and the satire that came out with all of the emotion that I never dreamed of before when I read the thing cold in print."

After school and on weekends, he and Ira spent hours listening to Gilbert and Sullivan operettas. They admired how the music and words worked together. Gilbert paid more attention to the words in songs than anyone they had ever heard before.

Yip began to write his own verses for the school newspaper and the neighborhood baseball team. He loved to see his name and his words in print. He had an English teacher who would notice something funny in a piece of Yip's writing. He'd ask Yip to read his piece to the class. "I'd read," said Yip, "and there would be twenty-odd kids laughing out loud, and, by God, that was really something. I'd tell myself, 'I want to repeat this experience!'"

Ira and Yip started a little newspaper called the *Daily Pass-It*, written on toilet paper. It had cartoons, puns, and imitations of other humor writing. They passed it around the classroom behind the teacher's back.

Yip and Ira studied classical poetry. Their writing was very disciplined. They learned poetic forms like the sonnet and the ballad. They were careful with the rhythm and length of their lines, and they were "never permitted to use . . . a tonal rhyme like home and tone." The rhymes had to be perfect and the meter had to fit exactly.

Yip and Gersh, as they called themselves, joined the school's official newspaper, the *Academic Herald*. Ira was art editor, and he and Yip started a humor column called "Much Ado." Later, at the City College of New York, they created a humor column called "Gargoyle Gargles." They wrote poems in different styles and forms about school life and events. Sometimes they wrote together, and they often offered helpful ideas about each other's work.

A life-long friendship was born on the Lower East Side. Ira and Yip continued to share rhymes, poems, songs, and a deep love of words for more than seventy years. Two of America's greatest lyricists had met through the coincidence of alphabetical seating.

Yip with friends from college.

CHAPTER 4

A Business Man Happily Goes Broke

Ira dropped out of college in 1916, but Yip couldn't afford to lose the opportunity for a good education. He kept studying, and suffering, with calculus and geometry. He was not a great student in many subjects, and he often sat in the back, writing poetry when he was supposed to be learning physics. But he had good classes, too. One professor kept Yip after class and encouraged him to keep writing, especially funny pieces.

Yip had some poems published, but he couldn't imagine that he could make a living writing. He said, "When I got out of college, I didn't pursue poetry . . . Nobody made a living at that. That's for fun, that's a sideline, you don't earn money that way, I used to think."

In 1918 Yip took a job in South America. He was glad to leave the United States to avoid fighting in World War I. Yip worked in a leather factory in Uruguay for over three years. He learned Spanish, and was successful at his job. The trip helped Yip grow up, and he was able to make enough money to support his father and mother. Yip still wrote, but business took most of his time.

When he returned, a friend offered him a partnership in a company selling electrical appliances. They incorporated their business as the Brooklyn Consolidated Gas and Iron Co. Yip worked hard and continued supporting his parents. Although his heart wasn't in his work, he was successful. He invented a metal ironing board and a clothes-drying rack that made a good profit for his company. "We made a lot of money," he said, "And I hated it . . . Being in business was something I detested. When I found that I could sell a song or a poem, I became me. I became alive."

Yip's poems were clever and funny. They were often about romance.

…My puritan training

Has taught me to spurn

Girl's lips; but unless I

Try, how shall I learn…

Or

In the Spring a young man's fancy

Lightly turns to thoughts of love,

And in Summer—and in Autumn—and

In Winter—see above.

Yip continued his friendship with Ira. They got together several times a week. Ira was beginning to write lyrics with his brother George, and Yip became aware of lyric writing as a profession.

At the time, the music business was very specialized. Usually, one person wrote lyrics, a different person wrote the music, and a singer or actor sang the song. The singer-songwriter who wrote, sang, and played his or her own songs was a rare concept.

Although lyric writing interested him, he loved the theater as a whole, music and all. "Business or no business, my first love in those heady days was still the theater. I went to all the musical shows and all the straight shows—I devoured them. The variety was staggering. There were something like sixty or seventy shows a season. There was a burst of enthusiasm, freshness, and new writers experimenting with new things. Rodgers and Hart, the Gershwins, Cole Porter, Kern and Hammerstein came on the scene with a whole new kind of song and show, far removed from Tin Pan Alley, more literate, more sparkling."

Tin Pan Alley was a few blocks in New York where publishers of popular songs had their businesses. Hundreds of writers churned out songs that could be sold as sheet music. Because radio stations didn't exist, and because so few people had phonographs, most people learned new songs from sheet music. Tin Pan Alley was filled with songwriters and song pluggers, musicians hired to play and sing the new songs, so that customers could decide what to buy. The music pouring out of the windows and doors was like listening to the racket of an army banging tin pans together. The image stuck in the name—Tin Pan Alley. Some songs made their way into Broadway revues, but the new style of writing for shows moved beyond Tin Pan Alley.

Yip went on to explain the difference. "The musical theater scene was quite a few steps removed from Tin Pan Alley. The people writing for it were well equipped. Most of them had college training . . . Mostly, the guys writing songs for Tin Pan Alley were close to illiterate grammatically, but they had a sense of showmanship and an ear for what the people liked."

Broadway is the area around Times Square in New York that was, and still is, the heart of the theater district. In 1880, Broadway became one of the first areas in the United States to have electric lighting when electric arc lamps were installed, which led to the nickname "The Great White Way." By the 1920s, theaters dotted the streets and people came from all over the country for theater performances. In 1927, 20,000,000 people attended Broadway shows. 250 shows opened that year and 50 were musicals. Broadway shows were booming.

Broadway was a booming place to work, too. Thousands of actors, singers, and dancers came to New York, hoping to get a part in a show. A lucky few would even become stars. But Broadway needed more than actors. Make-up artists, costume designers, set builders, stage managers, and lighting technicians all helped to create the magical atmosphere of the theater. Musicians accompanied songs. Choreographers created dance routines. Directors shaped the acting, singing and overall performance, and producers came up with the money, backing shows in hopes of creating a hit.

These days, when we watch a musical like *Mary Poppins* or *Lion King* we take for granted that the songs help tell the story, but it wasn't always true. Between 1915 and 1930, the nature of musical theater itself was changing.

Broadway shows with music were originally either revues or comic operettas. Revues were simply a series of sketches that included songs, without much connection between the meaning of the lyrics and the progression of the plot. Operettas told sentimental stories with exotic sets and fancy costumes. The music was classically based, with little attention to lyrics.

In 1927 a new musical, *Show Boat*, marked a revolutionary change in the way songs contributed to shows, and it raised the importance of songwriters. Written by Jerome Kern and Oscar Hammerstein II, *Show Boat* was not an operetta or a revue. It told one story, and the songs were critical to that story. *Show Boat's* songs were based in popular styles, but Hammerstein's music and Kern's lyrics had sophistication beyond most Tin Pan Alley songs.

"People began for the first time to listen to the lyrics in American musicals the way they had to Gilbert and Sullivan," said one writer. "The critics realized that here were lyrics worthy of attention . . . the words themselves might have entertainment value," added Ira Gershwin. Yip knew Jerome Kern and Oscar Hammerstein II, and he appreciated the change that they were creating.

Yip loved theater, but he was occupied with his work and family. In 1923, Yip married Alice Richmond. They had two children, Ernest and Marge. Yip changed his last name from Hochberg to Harburg at his wife's request: Alice thought that "Hoch" sounded like spitting. Yip worked to support his family, but Yip's sister remembered that he would sit and write verses during the day when he should have been working.

Yip lost his appliance business as America began losing its way. In 1929, the Great Depression hit the country, and his business went bankrupt. Yip lost $250,000, and was $50,000 in debt. Yip insisted on repaying his creditors, although it took him over ten years to do so.

For years, Ira Gershwin had been encouraging him to move to a career in songwriting, and Yip had begun to work with others on songs for shows. When his business went bankrupt, he decided to commit fully to his writing.

"All I had left was my pencil," he said. "I immediately got a hold of Ira and said, 'Ira, I think I'd like to be a songwriter from here on. I'm through with business.'" Ira was delighted. He loaned Yip some money and introduced him to a composer named Jay Gorney, with whom Yip began to work as he learned the craft of writing songs for musical theater.

As Yip started this new life, he sent his family to live with his sister Anna in Brooklyn. He moved into a small hotel room and found a job at a watch factory. He worked all day and wrote lyrics at night, often until three in the morning.

All around him, the economy was crumbling. Although he was in a difficult financial situation and his life had turned upside-down, Yip was excited about the change. He later said, sarcastically, "I had my fill of the dreamy, abstract thing called business, and I decided to face the harsh reality of writing lyrics for musical theatre."

He saw a rainbow in what seemed like a dark, grey sky.

Yip with his children, Ernest and Marge.

CHAPTER 5

Learning the Craft

Yip set out to learn how to write song lyrics. He was inspired by writers like Larry Hart, Cole Porter, and his good friend Ira Gershwin. Yip knew that writing a poem wasn't the same as writing a good song lyric. He said, "Verse [poetry] writing is . . . intellectual. A song done in a theater is an emotional explosion . . . You've got to move an audience, not only with the words, but with the emphasis on the music."

Yip wasn't left to himself to learn. He and Ira spent hours analyzing songs and writing together. Yip was also part of a group of writers who were in the inner circle of musical theater in New York. He remembered that time.

"Starting in the 1920s and continuing through the 1930s we got together almost every night, often at the Gershwins, where there were two pianos and we could play everything we had written that week and see how it went over. The others gave you criticism or an idea—there was a real camaraderie . . . We all wrote for each other and inspired each other. You wanted to come up every week with something worthwhile . . . there was a kind of healthy competition among us. You would not dare to write a bad rhyme or a clichéd tune."

Yip had a lot to learn. Writing song lyrics is a demanding and precise skill. Ira described what was required in a good lyricist. "A fondness for music, a feeling for rhyme, a sense of whimsy and humor, an eye for the balanced sentence, an ear for the current phrase, and the ability to imagine oneself a performer trying to put over the number in progress."

In addition to using language well, a lyricist has to work harmoniously with others. Most theater songs were written by two different people, a lyricist and a composer. One worked on the words, the other on the music. Some writers like Cole Porter or Irving Berlin did both and worked alone, but songwriting teams were far more common.

Yip understood the importance of collaboration, and he was good at it. Many years later, in 1967, he worked with a composer named Jule Styne on a musical called *Darling of the Day*. Jule talked about working with Yip. "He's a very easy fellow to work with, because when two people are working, if they both have a mutual respect, then you're secure, and you can say, 'Yip, I don't like that word' . . . He says, 'We'll get another word.' With his big pencil and that big sheet of paper. He'll give you another word. Want another note? I'll give you another note . . . That's when you know where you are."

Ira had introduced Yip to composer Jay Gorney, and they began to write together. Yip said that Jay taught him his first important lessons about blending words and music.

"The composer has to more or less feed you. Feeding him an idea, a title, is fine, but if you give him a complete . . . lyric first, usually a banal melody results. A great song requires a great composer, and a great composer brings out the best in a lyricist."

Yip and Jay began by writing songs for a radio show and for several different Broadway revues. Jay Gorney worked for Paramount's east coast movie studio. He and Yip wrote songs for movies and even cartoons. Yip also wrote some spoken verse pieces for cartoons.

But Yip wasn't the kind of writer who wanted to work with only one person. Between 1929 and 1934, he worked with over thirty different composers. In fact, over the span of his career, he worked with a greater number of different composers—over 60—than almost any other lyricist of that time. From the start, he described himself as a chameleon. "I always liked trying a new style. I love putting myself into everyone else's shoes, and each composer lends me a new pair."

Yip kept a notebook for ideas. "A good lyric writer has ideas stacked away," he said. "You store away titles, maybe one word you like." Yip's son Ernest remembers going to a movie with Yip. In the middle of laughing at the show, Yip pulled out a notebook to jot down an idea.

In 1930, Yip had his first hit, "I'm Yours" written with Johnny Green. He was learning fast, and working with many different composers gave him lots of exposure. Two years later he had more songs in Broadway shows than any other lyricist.

In 1932, Yip was hired to write lyrics for a new show called *Americana*. The show was intended to be about the nation's situation in the Great Depression. "It was the first such show with social comment," said Yip, and that energized his writing. Yip brought in several composers to work with him, and hired another lyric writer, Johnny Mercer, to help as well. Johnny Mercer went on to write many hits, including "That Old Black Magic," "Moon River," and "Autumn Leaves."

Johnny Mercer remembered what he learned from Yip. "He'll sit in a room all day and he'll dig and he'll dig and he'll dig . . . If we had to write four verses, he'd write eight . . . He was a big influence in teaching me how hard to work . . . Sometimes we'd get a rhyming dictionary and a [thesaurus] and we'd *sweat*."

Yip was working hard and having success with many composers. But *Americana* gave him the opportunity to write his first great and memorable song.

CHAPTER 6

Brother, Can You Spare a Dime?

From 1929 through the early 1940s, the United States and most of the world suffered from tremendous economic hardship during a time known as the Great Depression. People lost their life savings when banks failed. Unemployment reached 25%—one out of every four workers couldn't find a job. Families lost their homes, and many took to the road looking for work. Thousands of hungry people stood in breadlines where food was given away. They ate at soup kitchens every day. By the end of 1931, in New York City alone it was estimated that 85,000 meals a day were served in the city's breadlines. The U.S. had never known such an economic collapse.

"It was a terrible time," said one depositor when he lost his life savings after a sudden bank failure. "You felt as though the bottom had dropped out of your life, and I guess the thing that bothered me most was the fact that there was no notice."

One boy discovered his father crying in the basement. "We had owned a small bakery that had failed . . . A little later we lost most of our savings at a local bank that went under . . . I guess the thought that (my father) wouldn't be able to buy enough coal to get us through the winter was just too much for (him) to take . . . Things would get worse for us later on . . . but for me the low point of the Depression will be always be the sight of my father that day, crying in the coal bin."

The writer Sherwood Anderson described typical Depression era scenes. "Men who are heads of families, creeping through the streets of American cities, eating from garbage cans: men turned out of the houses and sleeping week after week on park benches, on the ground in parks, in the mud under bridges . . . Our streets are filled with beggars, with men new to the art of begging." Women shared this suffering.

People built shelters of packing crates, newspaper, and tin cans. These shantytowns were called Hoovervilles to mock the president, Herbert Hoover, who many people blamed for the Depression. Hoovervilles sprouted in New York, Chicago, Seattle, Denver, and most major American cities.

Children suffered most from hunger, cold and sickness.

In 1928, lyricist Jack Yellen and composer Milton Ager wrote a song for a Broadway revue called *Rain or Shine*. One night, Yellen passed the song out to musicians at a New York City hotel. The lead singer looked out at the somber audience and laughed when he read the lyrics, but he sang it anyway. "Sing it for the corpses," he said, sensing the gloom most people felt. The audience joined in, although they sang, in Yellen's words, "hysterically, liked doomed prisoners on their way to the firing squad."

The song was "Happy Days are Here Again." The lyrics were about clear skies and cheerfulness.

For most people, the song was ironic and funny because the lyrics were the opposite of the actual lives they led.

On Broadway, other shows and popular songs also ignored the condition of the country. Tunes like "Happy Days are Here Again" and "Wrap Your Troubles in Dreams (And Dream Your Troubles Away)" offered images of good times and prosperity, even as the whole country suffered. "Life is Just a Bowl of Cherries," by Ray Henderson, Buddy G. DeSylva, and Lew Brown, implied that money didn't matter. Irving Berlin's "Let's Have Another Cup of Coffee" advised people to go out and shop, an odd suggestion when so few people had extra money.

Maybe audiences wanted to be distracted from their problems and wanted to hear about promises of a better life. Some producers and songwriters were afraid to present songs that gave a realistic but disturbing view of the country's situation, fearing that audiences would stay away. As Mel Brooks later said, "Musicals sell optimism. Your dreams come true when you go to a show on Broadway. You go back to the Bronx and your dreams don't come true."

Americana was intended to be a different kind of show, one that didn't ignore the country's difficulties. Yip was hard at work on *Americana*. In addition to Jay Gorney, Yip also wrote with composers Harold Arlen and Burton Lane, both of whom would later become long-term writing partners.

As Yip walked through New York at the height of the Great Depression, a common greeting was "Can you spare a dime?" So many unemployed people were constantly asking for help. Yip took the greeting and made it the title of a song, but he wasn't sure what approach to follow in writing it.

Jay Gorney had a melody based on an old Russian lullaby. He had previously used it for a love song that hadn't been successful. Yip heard it and asked if he could come up with new words.

Yip's first idea was to make the song an attack on rich people who had so much money while others had nothing. Gradually, though, the focus of the song shifted and Yip wrote about people who were suffering. He remembered crying as he wrote and having to stop because he was overcome with feeling. However, he didn't want to write a song about just misery or about only asking for a handout. In the end, the song became about asking questions.

Yip said, "I grew up when America had a dream, and its people a hope . . . The dream collapsed. The system fell apart. This was a good country, on its way to greatness. It had given our immigrants more freedom, more education, more opportunity than they had ever known. What happened? . . . In the song, the man is really saying: I made an investment in this country. It doesn't reduce him to a beggar. It makes him a dignified human being . . . and a bit outraged, too, as he should be . . . I built the railroad, I built the tower, I went to war for this country. Why are my hands empty? . . . [the song asks] the universal question of 'why does the man who produces not share in the wealth?'"

Brother Can You Spare A Dime?

They used to tell me I was building a dream, and so I followed the mob,

When there was earth to plow, or guns to bear, I was always there right on the job.

They used to tell me I was building a dream, with peace and glory ahead,

Why should I be standing in line, just waiting for bread?

Once I built a railroad, I made it run, made it race against time.

Once I built a railroad; now it's done. Brother, can you spare a dime?

Once I built a tower, up to the sun, brick, and rivet, and lime;

Once I built a tower, now it's done. Brother, can you spare a dime?

Once in khaki suits, gee, we looked swell,

Full of that Yankee Doodly Dum,

Half a million boots went slogging through Hell,

And I was the kid with the drum!

Say, don't you remember, they called me Al; it was Al all the time.

Say, don't you remember, I'm your pal? Buddy, can you spare a dime?

Once in khaki suits, gee, we looked swell,

Full of that Yankee Doodly Dum,

Half a million boots went slogging through Hell,

And I was the kid with the drum!

Say, don't you remember, they called me Al; it was Al all the time.

Say, don't you remember, I'm your pal? Buddy, can you spare a dime?

When Jay and Yip finished the song the show's producer had doubts but agreed to include it.

From *Americana's* opening night, the song was a smash success. It was the first theater, film, or popular song that addressed the suffering of the Depression directly. One critic said it "expressed the spirit of these times with more heartbreaking anguish than any of the prose bards of the day." Americana itself was not reviewed so favorably; another critic found the song to be the only good thing in the whole show.

The song took off. Bing Crosby and Rudy Vallee, two very popular singers, made recordings that sold in huge quantities. Bands everywhere played it. Some radio stations refused to play the song, considering it to be too political, or maybe just too serious. Their refusal didn't matter; soon everyone knew "Brother, Can You Spare A Dime?" Yip was suddenly in demand for interviews and theater job offers.

Yip learned something about the power of songs. Many years later he said, "The song became such a hit and such an expression of the whole era that it dawned on me that communication through song is probably the most powerful way of teaching people, and I decided that from there on whatever I wrote was going to have something to do with the human condition . . . Songs have been the not-so-secret weapon behind every fight for freedom, every struggle against injustice and bigotry: 'The Marseillaise,' 'The Battle Hymn of the Republic,' 'We Shall Overcome,' and many more. Give me the makers of the songs of a nation and I care not who makes the laws."

Yip wanted to write great songs. He also wanted to express his political views. In "Brother, Can You Spare A Dime?" his two ambitions came together into one brilliant and powerful anthem that touched millions of people, not just in America, but around the world for many years to come.

CHAPTER 7
The Hits Keep Coming

In "Brother, Can You Spare a Dime?" Yip had a major hit. The song also marked a step in his evolution of learning the craft of writing lyrics.

Yip continued to write with different composers, each of whom brought out a different aspect of his work. One of Yip's partners was Vernon Duke. Vernon was from Russia, and he had been trained in the sophisticated classical music tradition. Yip and Vernon were different kinds of personalities, and they only worked together for four years, between 1930 and 1934. Yip said that working with Vernon allowed him to focus on humorous songs. One example of their collaboration is "That's Life" written for a Broadway show in 1932 called *Walk a Little Faster*.

That's Life

That's Life

St. Peter blows on his horn

And so you wake up one morn

Find that you're born

That's Life.

That's Life

You buy a pair of long pants

For that fraternity dance

Bingo! Romance.

That's Life.

That's Life

You go to school and learn La Paloma

And Greek for corn on the cob.

Then you get your diploma

And you're right in line for that Fuller Brush job.

That's Life

You're right on top of the heap

You get a swell penthouse cheap

Walk in your sleep

That's Life.

That's Life

You go along in the red

Just when you think you're getting ahead.

Bingo! You're dead.

That's Life.

"That's Life" is funny, but it's about serious subjects, life, death, and the fleeting nature of happiness. The song gets its humor from its tone. It sounds like a regular guy talking, like cheap philosophy on a street corner. "You do this, you do that, you get this." The form of three rhyming lines also keeps the listener a little off balance, adding to the humor. Audiences unconsciously expect rhyming lines in even numbers.

Although the show was only mildly successful, Yip and Vernon Duke wrote another song for it called "April in Paris." Since Yip had never been to Paris, he went to a travel agent and got some brochures to spark his imagination. "April in Paris" became an American classic and was recorded by many jazz artists. Two years later Universal Pictures asked Yip to develop a whole movie based on the song.

April in Paris

(Verse)

April's in the air,

But here in Paris

April wears a diff'rent gown.

You can see her waltzing

Down the street.

The tang of wine is in the air,

I'm drunk with all the happiness

That spring can give.

Never dreamed it could be so

Exciting to live.

(Chorus)

April in Paris

Chestnut in blossoms

Holiday tables under the trees.

April in Paris

This is a feeling

No one can ever reprise.

I never knew the charm of Spring

Never met it face to face.

I never knew my heart could sing

Never missed a warm embrace,

'Til

April in Paris

Whom can I run to?

What have you done to

My heart?

Critics recognized Yip's talent. The New York Times ran a profile on him in 1933, calling Yip a "member of the newer school of lyric writers who are giving Broadway audiences these days a series of rhymes more intelligent than 'June' and 'moon.'" And Billboard magazine wrote that William Shakespeare was the most prolific playwright, but E.Y. Harburg turned out the largest number of lyrics.

The team of Yip and Vernon Duke didn't last. Their personalities clashed too much to collaborate further. At the same time, Yip's marriage ended in divorce.

In 1932, Yip began to work with composer Harold Arlen. Yip was asked to write a song for a show called "The Great Magoo." He asked Harold to work with him, and the result was another classic, "It's Only a Paper Moon."

It's Only a Paper Moon

I never feel a thing is real

When I'm away from you

Out of your embrace

The world's a temporary parking place.

Mmm, mm, mm, mm

A bubble for a minute

Mmm, mm, mm, mm

You smile, the bubble has a rainbow in it.

Say, it's only a paper moon

Sailing over a cardboard sea

But it wouldn't be make-believe

If you believed in me.

Yes, it's only a canvas sky

Hanging over a muslin tree

But it wouldn't be make-believe

If you believed in me.

Without your love

It's a honky-tonk parade

Without your love

It's a melody played in a penny arcade.

It's a Barnum and Bailey world

Just as phony as it can be

But it wouldn't be make-believe

If you believed in me.

Many of Yip's lyrics are about believing in illusions or about the shattering of those illusions. He felt that people needed to be careful in what they believed; believing could lead to disappointment. At the same time, he thought that love between two people could be an answer to how to live happily. He believed that true love was not an illusion, but a real possibility.

Yip began to work extensively with Harold Arlen. On a show called *Life Begins at 8:40*, Yip and Ira Gershwin wrote together as lyricists. Yip recalled their work on that show. "We got together every night at 9 or 10 o'clock and worked 'til 4 in the morning, with Harold at the piano, and it was joyous."

Ira was known as "the jeweler" for his ability to set words into musical phrases. He and Yip had a similar approach to lyrics: precise, witty, and playful with language. "Two very interesting guys," said Harold Arlen, "always experimenting with words. Using the language, twisting it, bending it."

Lyric writing and poetry are not the same as prose; there's more meaning packed into the words of a poem or a song. "For me the task is never to say the thing directly, and yet to say it—to think in a curve, so to speak," said Yip. "Tell all the truth," said the poet Emily Dickinson about writing, "but tell it slant." Good writing needs to show new directions or approaches, even if it's about an old idea.

One of the songs, "Fun to be Fooled," shows Yip's ongoing thinking about believing in illusions. The phrase was a popular advertising slogan, and Yip made it the center of a song.

Fun to be Fooled.

Fun to pretend.

Fun to believe

That love is unending,

Thought I was done

Still it is fun

Being fooled again.

Harold was a dedicated composer. "He was frightened of everything sounding like something else," said Yip. "He will labor on one phrase, sometimes for weeks exploring every musical possibility with the patience of a chess champion."

Yip had found a composer who he loved to work with. He said, "Harold was one of the rare guys who (could go) from fun to high misery or comedy . . . and make the tune fit the idea . . . He really has genius qualities." Over the next five years, most of Yip's published songs were written with Harold Arlen.

When the show opened in August of 1934, it received rave reviews. One writer said, "Harburg's arrival on the musical comedy and revue scene several years ago added a new vigor to lyric writing . . . [In Life Begins at 8:40] he managed to sneak in several numbers which had a strong satiric and social import and which somehow got under the skin of his audiences."

Not only was the show a success, but it marked the first time that Yip had worked with Bert Lahr, a comic actor whose style fit Yip's sensibilities. Ray Bolger was in the show, too. Five years later, they would all work together again. Bert Lahr would play the part of the Cowardly Lion and Ray Bolger, the part of the Scarecrow in *The Wizard of Oz*.

CHAPTER 8

Hollywood

The first movies were made in New York in the 1890s. They told simple stories and used a variety of early projection and production techniques. Because movies had no sound, live musicians accompanied them, usually on a piano or an organ.

In 1910, D.W. Griffith shot the first Hollywood movie. The industry was young and still centered in New York, but by 1915, Los Angeles passed New York, and Hollywood became the leader of American filmmaking.

Movie studios soon covered large blocks of land in and around Hollywood. Movie stars, directors, and producers bought glamorous houses and basked beside swimming pools in California's glorious climate. As movies and movie theaters expanded, Hollywood became world famous as the center of this new art form. The first feature length film hit with synchronized dialogue is generally considered to be *The Jazz Singer* in 1927.

The evolution of film musicals in Hollywood was similar to that of theater musicals in New York. Once films featured sound, most songs were simply an opportunity to showcase a singer or a fancy dance routine. The songs didn't really connect to the plot or the characters. With few exceptions, songs could easily be interchanged from movie to movie, without noticing much difference. Films that relied on songs for story development were rare.

Hollywood producers saw songwriters as cogs in the machine of movie making, no more important than make-up artists or camera operators. Producers showed little respect for them as artists. On Broadway, songwriters helped develop the shows, giving feedback and writing new material as needed. In Hollywood, they wrote songs and picked up a paycheck. The producers and directors used what they needed and threw out the rest. Songwriters felt no ownership or ongoing relationship to a production.

In the early 1930s, many Broadway songwriters, including Oscar Hammerstein, Jerome Kern, and the Gershwins, went west to Hollywood looking for work. The Depression hit Broadway hard, and attendance and revenues were down. In 1934, there were only 14 new Broadway musicals. Hollywood promised good pay and excellent weather, but the atmosphere was not the same.

Harold Arlen put it bluntly. "We had no prestige." Even George Gershwin, the best known of them all, wasn't respected. "He'd be invited to a party and be expected to sit down and play like a hired entertainer."

Yip came to Hollywood in 1934, where he worked on developing a script from his song "April in Paris." After a few months, Universal Studios dropped the project. Yip and Harold Arlen signed a contract with Warner Brothers Studios to write songs for their movies.

One of the songs they wrote was called "Last Night When We Were Young." The sadness of the lyrics may have reflected events in Yip's life of the last few years—his marriage ending, the death of his father, and even the loss of his business.

Last Night When We Were Young (excerpt)

Last night when we were young

Love was a star, a song unsung

Life was so new, so real, so right

Ages ago, last night.

Today the world is old

You went away and time grew cold

Where is that star that seemed so bright

Ages ago, last night.

At first, Yip missed the vibrant atmosphere of New York and the respect given to songwriters there, but he soon fell under the California spell. He lived in a house designed by Frank Lloyd Wright with a swimming pool. Yip had never lived in such a luxurious place. "Sunshine, sunshine, every day, everywhere. Shorts, tennis, golf, swimming, kumquats." It was a long way from New York's Lower East Side tenements. Ira wrote to Yip asking, "So you've learned to like California? What's new about that?"

Songwriters still shared a sense of camaraderie. They gathered to sing and share their work just as they had in New York. Yip remembered that time.

"We always worried about what our colleagues would think of this thing and we were really ashamed of ourselves if we had one thing that sounded like something else or that wasn't original . . . If Harold Arlen would say, 'This sounds like [Cole] Porter,' he would throw that tune in the basket."

In the 1930s, Yip went back and forth between Hollywood and New York, working on movies in California and musicals on Broadway.

In 1937, he created a Broadway show called *Hooray for What!* which became a immediate smash hit. Yip had come up with the idea, helped to shape the script, and written the songs with Harold Arlen. *Hooray for What!* had an anti-war message; once again, Yip had brought social commentary to Broadway.

Yip couldn't turn his back on the issues he thought were important. He later said, "The lyricist, like any other artist, cannot be neutral. He should be committed to the side of humanity. He should be concerned for the rights, potential, and dignity of his fellow man."

Hooray for What! included a song called "In the Shade of the New Apple Tree." It wasn't a major song in the show, but a producer for MGM pictures named Arthur Freed heard it and decided that the style and feeling of the song were just what he wanted for a new project he was developing. The music captured feelings of family oriented entertainment, while the lyrics had a sense of swinging and coolness that would appeal to modern audiences. Freed thought that this would be the perfect mix for *The Wizard of Oz.*

"That song got us *The Wizard of Oz*," said Harold Arlen. "There were plenty of other songwriters who were unhappy and shocked when they heard that we'd gotten it, because they'd all been sitting around, waiting for that job." Although Yip and Harold Arlen had worked in Hollywood, they were a surprising choice for *The Wizard of Oz*, because other songwriters were better known.

Yip suggested to Freed that the movie have a fully integrated score, where the songs, the story, and the dancing all worked together. Not only would Yip and Harold be able to write songs for this highly anticipated movie project, but they would also have the chance to work closely with the development of the plot and characters

Although we now take this approach for granted in musicals, in 1938 only a few musicals had used this method. "I loved the idea of having the freedom to do lyrics that were not just songs but were scenes," said Yip. Yip had a golden opportunity with this movie. He became more than the lyricist; in the end, he became the script editor and the one who shaped the overall story.

Yip Harburg and Harold Arlen were hired on May 19, 1938 for a fee of $25,000, which in today's dollars would be about $400,000 dollars. They only had fourteen weeks to write the songs. They took the keys to a bungalow at the movie studio and got to work.

L: Harold Arlen and his dog Pan; R: Yip Harburg. Working together in Beverly Hills, 1935.

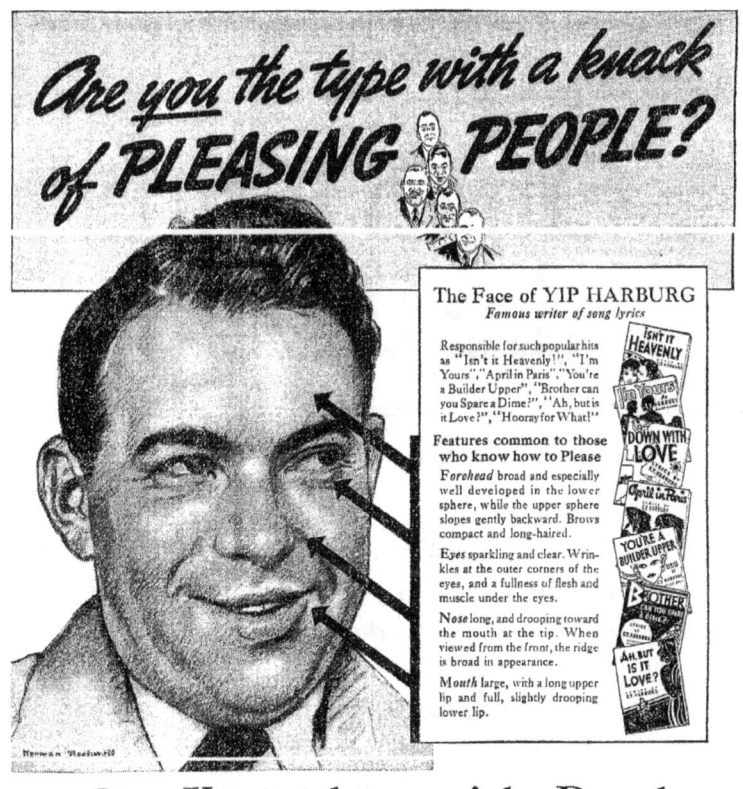

An ad from 1938 designed by artist Norman Rockwell featuring Yip.

CHAPTER 9

Off to Write the Wizard

The 1939 press release for *The Wizard of Oz* gives some idea of the size and scope of the movie. "More than 165 arts and crafts were represented in the making of the picture, including workers never before used in a production. There were glass workers, color mixers, cellophane experts, flower makers, a sky writer, powder and fire men, magicians to invent new tricks, high voltage electrical experts, water tinters, beard dyers, wig makers, men who painted pictures with felt strips, lighting men, animal trainers, prospective artists, strange noise developers, hedge trimmers, and dozens of others . . . For the picture a total of 33,210 costumes were designed and made, 8,428 separate make-ups were sketched in color and applied to faces, sixty-five fantastic settings built from 1,020 separate units, 212,180 individual sounds were placed in the picture, and eighty-four different effects created for the unusual events of Oz."

Filmed from October 1938 to March 1939, *The Wizard of Oz* was a technical masterpiece, pushing the edges of filmmaking abilities and processes. It was one of the first live-action movies to be shot in color. Although the publicity above inflates the figures, the size of the production still makes the movie memorable for its time. The novel effects and ideas guaranteed that audiences would be intrigued by the visuals. The nearly three million dollars it cost to make and publicize the film was at the upper end for movie budgets in 1939.

L. Frank Baum's "The Wonderful Wizard of Oz" had been published in 1900. It sold 10,000 copies in its first two weeks, which was a huge sales figure for the time. It quickly became popular throughout the country. Many critics now call it the first uniquely American fairy tale, with its classic themes and characters, and settings like cornfields, tin men, and scarecrows.

Before he died in 1919, Baum wrote thirteen more books about Oz. The books were in so much demand that nineteen more titles appeared in the 1920s and 30s, written by Ruth Plumly Thompson.

The popularity of the book soon led to a theatrical show. In 1903 a stage musical ran for 300 performances on Broadway and toured throughout the country for the next ten years. This Broadway musical was made up of songs from so many different composers that no one publisher could put out a score. Two silent movie versions and a cartoon adaptation also preceded the 1939 Oz film that we now know.

Each of these earlier shows influenced the film, but Disney's *Snow White and the Seven Dwarfs* had a big impact, too. Released in 1938, Snow White was the first full-length animated film. Walt Disney's wife had tried to talk him out of making the movie, saying, "No one's ever gonna pay a dime to see a dwarf picture." Disney went ahead with his plans. The movie received a standing ovation at its first showing and went on to make four times more money than any other film that year.

The producers and writers of *The Wizard of Oz* used some of the same elements that were present in Snow White: An evil queen/witch, marching songs ("Heigh Ho, Heigh Ho" and "We're Off to See the Wizard"), poison (apples and poppies), magic seeing tools (the queen's mirror and the witch's crystal ball) and funny, small people (the dwarves and munchkins.) The writers weren't trying to copy *Snow White* but they did want to build on some of the same ideas, hoping to attract a similar kind and size of audience.

In 1939, M.G.M. Studios was producing movies at the rate of one every nine days. No one at the studio was counting on *The Wizard of Oz* to make much money; it was a prestige film, designed to attract attention to the studio for innovation and quality, even if it didn't bring in huge audiences. "They didn't think they were going to make any money with the picture," Yip said later, but they hoped it would receive many Academy Award nominations. Still, if *The Wizard of Oz* did draw audiences like *Snow White* had, so much the better.

Arthur Freed was an associate producer on *The Wizard of Oz*, but he ended doing much of the hands-on work in the movie. He was a songwriter originally, but now he was more interested in the bigger job of shaping whole movies.

Arthur Freed and Yip Harburg were radically different people. Freed was politically conservative and was grounded in studio politics and business. Yip's politics were left wing, and, as scriptwriter Noel Langley said, "Yip was out of Alice in Wonderland . . . He thought he should correct [this planet] so we could all lead ideal lives."

Still, they respected each other, even though they disagreed over politics. Freed never seriously considered anyone besides Yip and Harold Arlen to write the songs.

Yip knew that Freed liked his work. "Freed felt my lyrics had a poetic value," he said. "The average producers didn't refer to it that way." Another songwriter, Harry Warren, added, "Freed was the only producer who understood anything about songwriters. He never said, 'I have to have the song by nine o'clock Wednesday.' The rest of the producers ordered a song like they were ordering a steak dinner."

The movie creation had a long history, with eleven script writers and four different directors all contributing to the final product. At the time, no one working on the movie realized that they were in the midst of creating a timeless masterpiece. "We didn't know it was a classic," said Tin Man Jack Haley. "We were getting paid, and it was a lot of weeks of steady work."

It was steady work and hard work, too. It took hours to apply the make-up and costumes for the Tin Man, the Scarecrow, and the Cowardly Lion. The outfits were hot and uncomfortable. The three men's appearances were considered so outrageous that they weren't allowed to eat in the studio cafeteria. Jack Haley (the Tin Man) had to have a special board to lean against during breaks, because his costume wouldn't allow him to sit down. And Margaret Hamilton, who played the witch, had her hand badly burned during the scene where she is writing "Surrender Dorothy" in the sky with her flaming broom.

Yip loved the book when he first read it, and he was passionate about keeping the essence of the story authentic, even if characters or plot events changed. In the end, Yip not only wrote the lyrics, but he also played a large and uncredited role in shaping the dialogue and story that would eventually become *The Wizard of Oz*. But first he and Harold had to write the songs.

L. Frank Baum's original book "The Wonderful Wizard of Oz" had no rainbow. Yip Harburg saw the need for a bridge between colorful Oz and Dorothy's everyday, black and white world of Kansas. He came up with the idea. "I'll put a rainbow in it," and history was made.

Yip singing with the cast of The Wizard of Oz *for a radio broadcast, "Good News" radio program rehearsal. Clockwise from top center: MGM executive LK Sidney, Yip, composer/conductor Meredith Willson, music publisher Harry Link, Harold Arlen, Judy Garland, Bert Lahr, Ray Bolger.*
June 26, 1939

CHAPTER 10

Over the Rainbow

Yip and Harold Arlen often worked at night, because they liked to play tennis and be outside in the California sun during the day.

They began their working sessions by talking about the emotion and meaning of a particular song. Harold would create a melody to go with the idea they had discussed, and Yip would come up with a title. Harold would finish the music, and then Yip would write the lyrics.

Harold Arlen often came up with melodies in his head. He didn't usually compose at the piano. He might be driving or playing golf, and suddenly, inspiration would strike. He'd grab a notebook and write down a melody line and later, take his idea to the piano.

Yip remembered the process. "He'd keep playing a [musical] line over and over until I learned it by heart. There was something about a composer playing a tune over and over for you. You couldn't get away from it." As Harold played, Yip began to hear words. Yip said, "If we were at Harold's house and ran into real problems, I'd go home and plant." He would turn lyrics around in his mind as he walked or worked in the garden, and eventually the song would take shape.

For *The Wizard of Oz*, Yip and Harold Arlen began by working on what they considered the easier songs. Yip found a tune that Harold had written but never used in *Hooray for What?* He used it for the lyrics of "If I Only Had a Brain/Heart/Nerve," three songs with identical music for which Yip's lyrics created three different characters.

Yip's worksheets from the song include some lines that didn't make it into the film. The Scarecrow's discarded lines include: I would be no sweet potato, I would think out things like Plato, and I could save any nation/ with orations on inflation. And the Lion never got to sing: I would be as good as others/ Good enough for Ringling Brothers.

"Ding, Dong, the Witch is Dead," "The Merry Old Land of Oz," and "King of the Forest" followed, as Yip and Harold developed songs that could be the foundation of scenes in the movie. "We're Off to See the Wizard" was created during the filming.

Although the process of writing the hit song "Over the Rainbow" proceeded in the same manner, Yip and Harold faced the added complication of a deadline. They were at the end of their contract. The song needed to be written and finished, and they didn't have it yet.

As usual, they began with a concept. "Yearning" was the word that best captured the idea of Dorothy and her troubled situation. Harold Arlen worked for weeks on creating a melody. Yip had given him an initial title of "I Want To Be On The Other Side of the Rainbow."

Harold Arlen couldn't create a melody he liked for the song. "I knew what I wanted, and I couldn't get it," he said. He became nervous and depressed.

When he went with his wife to see a movie at the famous Grauman's Chinese Theatre, Harold was too anxious to drive. Suddenly, the melody came to him. He told his wife to stop the car so he could write it down.

Harold went home and played the musical phrase on the piano. At midnight, when he had developed the idea further and was satisfied, he called Yip to come hear it. Yip came right over. However, Harold played it loud with big chords, like a one-man orchestra. Yip thought it was too bold for a young girl to sing.

"My heart fell," Yip said. "My first reaction was 'Oh no, not for little Dorothy.'" Harold Arlen was disappointed. He thought he had a tune that would work. He kept working on it, and two weeks later Harold and Yip asked Ira Gershwin to come over and offer a second opinion.

When Ira arrived, he listened. Then he asked Harold to play the song more simply, like a pop song. Suddenly, the song transformed from an overpowering feeling to something gentle and wistful. With this new approach, they all agreed that the melody would do well for the song.

At Yip's urging, Harold wrote the middle part, where the lyrics would eventually be "Someday I'll wish upon a star." Yip later said that the two notes alternating in the melody echoed the tune Harold used to call his dog, but Arlen said it came from a children's music book.

Now Yip had to write the words. He remembered the initial image of a young girl in trouble. He saw that her "life is messed up, Where do I run? The song has to be full of childish pleasures. Of lemon drops . . . Kansas is an arid place, no color in her life, flowers don't even grow . . . The only colorful thing Dorothy saw, occasionally, would be the rainbow . . . If I were a child that's where I'd want to be . . . I Want to Be on the Other Side of the Rainbow was my title . . . But he gave me a tune with those first two notes. I tried 'I'll go over the rainbow someday' and 'Someday over the rainbow.' I had difficulty coming to the idea of Somewhere. For a while I thought I would just leave those two notes out."

Yip talked about his approach to the words. "You have to work for sound and the emotion of the tune . . . [for "Over the Rainbow"] I was given a tune which, for the first part, I couldn't use consonants . . . You have to use open vowels. 'Somewhere over the Rainbow' the 'o' comes right in—that's an important part of the writing . . . the sound has importance. 'skies are blue' 'way up high.'"

"Over the Rainbow" and "Brother, Can You Spare a Dime?" share some common themes. Both songs start low and sweep up the scale, descending slowly over the next two lines. The rising melody illustrates the idea of the dreams in the words, and the falling melody brings the singer back to reality. Both songs are also framed by questions, a common technique that Yip used. "Brother, can you spare a dime?" and "Why, oh, why can't I?" both show a narrator who can't understand why they are separated from their dream.

Freed, Yip, and Harold had to fight to keep the song in the movie. Yip said that Freed in particular pleaded, shouted, and used all the force of his friendship with studio head L.B. Mayer to keep the song. In the end, the song remained. And it became one of the most recognized and loved songs in the world.

Yip added, "We were just doing work, earning a living, and liking what we were doing. We never thought of posterity." Harold Arlen added, "I knew 'Over the Rainbow' was a strong song, but I never knew its true strength until afterward."

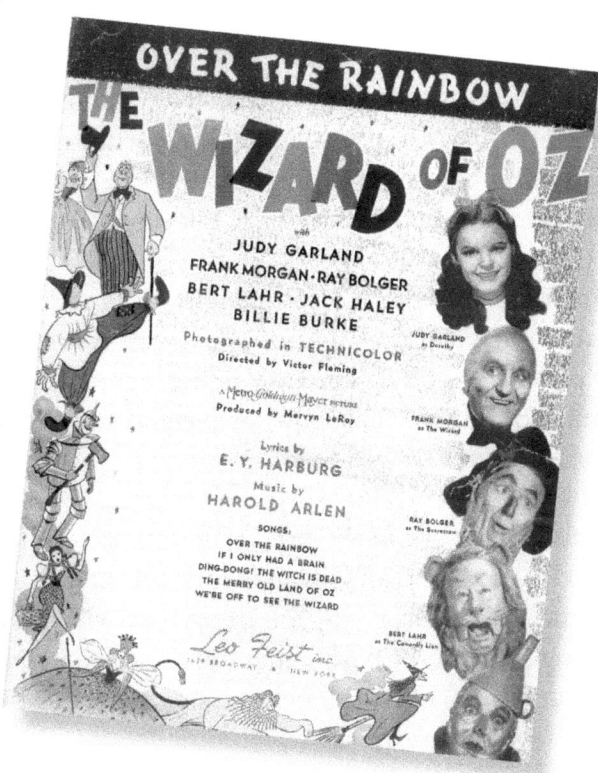

CHAPTER 11

Script Doctor

The script for *The Wizard of Oz* had more than ten writers. Ideas were passed back and forth. Scenes were cut, added, and then cut again. Four different directors oversaw the shooting. Through it all, Yip Harburg helped shape the final script, trying to keep Baum's fairy tale alive.

One of the primary scriptwriters, Noah Langley, was angry when his ideas were taken out of one version. Yip interceded with studio executives, and Langley's script was restored. Langley remembered later, "In the end, Harburg became so militant that Freed (a producer) supported him. If it hadn't been for Harburg going to Freed and blowing his top . . ."

Yip knew what would work in the movie, and he fought for it. "I said to Arthur Freed, 'Give me time and let me work the thing out lyrically and musically. Let me write a score for the thing that will tell the story, and then we will hang some of the best scenes onto that score.' Now that was a completely maverick way of working, but I thought it was the musical feel that was going to swing this show."

Because the movie intended to connect the songs with the script and the characters, Yip's help was essential. "Songs seem simple," he said. "They're not. The process of putting music in is very intricate. The function of a song is to simplify everything, to take the clutter out of too much plot and too many characters, to telescope everything into one emotional idea. You have to throw out the unnecessary. And lots of things not in the script have to be invented to make the songs work."

Yip wrote the lyrics and the spoken dialogue to Munchkinland. The songs were recorded by Hollywood singers on a tape recorder created just for the purpose of recording them and then speeding up their singing, which created the unforgettable high-pitched sound of the Munchkins.

One of Yip's major additions was near the end, where the Wizard gives out a diploma, a medal, and a testimonial, but he shaped the whole movie as he worked with scriptwriters. He recalled, "I liked a lot of things Langley had done and threw the other stuff out. I clarified the story. I edited the whole thing and brought back Langley's story, which was simpler. And I added my own." In the ending, Yip emphasized one of his major themes—that the symbols of society are silly because the reality of who we are is inside us.

Yip also suggested that Bert Lahr, an actor whose roots were in vaudeville, play the Cowardly Lion. He knew how funny and also how emotional Bert could be in a role that required humor and feeling.

Yip remembered working with Judy Garland. "She was an instinctive artist. She could learn a song faster than anybody I've ever seen. She could sit down beside Harold at the piano bench while he played a song through and learn it right then . . . And she could dance and she could clown . . . She was completely professional." "Over the Rainbow" would go on to define Judy Garland's career.

Yip worked at the film set day after day. "All a director had to do was follow the lyrics," he said. But he was there to make sure the director followed those lyrics to the right ending. Yip had a freedom and an influence over the movie that was unheard of for lyricists.

Yip had influence, but not control. He wanted the song in the poppy fields to be longer, but the director shortened it. The director removed a dance sequence to a song called "The Jitterbug." Yip also didn't like the ending. He thought it was too sentimental. And the decision to include "Over the Rainbow" was out of his hands. In the Hollywood world, songwriters were not at the top of the command chain.

The movie premiered in Oconomowoc, Wisconsin on August 12, 1939, and in Los Angeles and New York a few days later. Many critics didn't like it. One called it "a stinkeroo . . . it displays no trace of good taste, or ingenuity." Another added, "The story has some lovely ideas . . . but it doesn't know what to do with them."

"Over the Rainbow" won an Academy Award for best song, but most of the Awards that year went to *Gone with the Wind*. The film didn't turn a profit for nearly ten years. However, when CBS bought it for an annual television showing, the movie took off. In its first year on television, 1956, an estimated 45 million people watched. The movie's popularity grew and spread through popular culture. It was only shown once a year, which was most people's only chance to see it, since there were no video players, DVDs, or internet streaming. In 1982, it was estimated that 49% of all American children watched that year's broadcast.

In the 1970s, Yip said, "I hadn't realized what an impact the picture makes on children all over the world until the last six or seven years."

The songs, the characters, and lines from the script are learned, repeated, and referred to in other movies, songs, books, and artwork. Dorothy's red shoes are the most viewed objects on display at the Smithsonian Museum. The musical *Wicked*, which reimagines *The Wizard of Oz*, has been a hit on Broadway and around the world since 2003.

Books and articles have been written about why this movie takes such deep hold on so many people. There's no single answer to that question, but the songs are an essential piece of the movie's success. The lyrics are clever, memorable, and easy to understand. The melodies are filled with hooks, which makes them catchy and easy to sing along with. The songs also fit into the story and the characters so perfectly that viewers are never distracted by transitions from music to speaking. The movie works as a whole piece and stays true to L. Frank Baum's vision, and for that, more than anyone else, we have Yip Harburg to thank.

CHAPTER 12

After the Wizard

After he finished working on the Wizard, Yip turned to other projects. He and Harold wrote "Lydia, the Tattooed Lady" for the Marx Brothers, which became a signature song for Groucho Marx.

Lydia, the Tattooed Lady

Ah, Lydia. She was the most glorious creature Under the su-un. Thais. DuBarry. Garbo. Rolled into one.

Lydia oh Lydia, say have you met Lydia? Lydia, the Tattooed Lady. She has eyes that folks adore so, And a torso even more so.

Lydia oh Lydia, that encyclopidia, Oh Lydia the Queen of Tattoo. On her back is the Battle of Waterloo. Beside it the wreck of the Hesperus, too. And proudly above waves the Red, White, and Blue, You can learn a lot from Lydia.

When her robe is unfurled, she will show you the world, If you step up and tell her where. For a dime you can see Kankakee or Paris, Or Washington crossing the Delaware.

Oh Lydia oh Lydia, say have you met Lydia? Oh Lydia the Tattooed Lady When her muscles start relaxin', Up the hill comes Andrew Jackson.

Lydia oh Lydia, that encyclopidia, Oh Lydia the queen of them all! For two bits she will do a mazurka in jazz, With a view of Niagara that nobody has. And on a clear day you can see Alcatraz. You can learn a lot from Lydia.

Come along and see Buff'lo Bill with his lasso. Just a little classic by

Mendel Picasso. Here is Captain Spaulding exploring the Amazon. Here's Godiva but with her pajamas on.

Here is Grover Whalen unveilin' the Trilon. Over on the West Coast we have Treasure Islan'. Here's Najinsky a-doin' the rhumba. Here's her social security numba.

In 1939, actresses were not even allowed to wear sweaters in movies; the movie censors thought that sweaters were too provocative. The censors did not like "Lydia" with its suggestive images of bare skin. Yip and Harold got past the censors by adding the last verse. When Lydia gets married, the whole situation becomes proper.

Oh Lydia, oh Lydia that encyclopidia, Oh Lydia the champ of them all. She once swept an Admiral clear off his feet. The ships on her hips made his heart skip a beat. And now the old boy's in command of the fleet, For he went and married Lydia.

Groucho Marx singing "Lydia" in the movie At the Circus.

Artists around the world have sung "Lydia." Jim Henson, the creator of the Muppets, said that it was his favorite song, and he featured it on the first Muppet Show. It was also sung at his funeral.

In 1940 Yip went back to Broadway to work on a show called *Hold on to Your Hats*. Harold Arlen was busy with another project, so Yip teamed up with composer Burt Lane. The show, featuring Al Jolson, a famous vaudeville and Broadway star, was a success, mostly because audiences wanted to see Al Jolson on stage. Critics praised the score, too.

Yip returned to Hollywood and spent several years working with Burt Lane, Harold Arlen, and other composers on songs for movies, none of which became huge hits. Yip had a house built, got remarried, and worked as a producer on a movie, *Meet the People*, which he had produced for the stage the year before.

He also wrote songs that reflected the patriotic feelings of the time. The United States was at war with Germany and Japan. Yip wrote songs like "Son of a Gun Who Picks on Uncle Sam" and "You Can Always Tell a Yank" in support of the war effort.

He and Harold wrote songs for a movie called *Cabin in the Sky*. *Cabin in the Sky* was the first Hollywood movie for a general audience that starred African-American actors and actresses.

The hit song in *Cabin in the Sky* was "Happiness is a Thing Called Joe."

It seem like Happiness is jes' a thing called Joe,

He's got a smile that makes the lilac wanna grow,

He's got a way that makes the

angels heave a sigh...

Yip talked about the importance of rhyme, especially internal rhyme, when he reflected on the lyrics to this song. "There was something I tried to do with that song which most laymen probably would never know about. When you're writing a song, where the rhyme falls makes it either hard or easy to remember. There are certain tricks that the skilled lyric writer has to make a song memorable, provided it doesn't become mechanical . . . In other words, you want to rhyme as many places as you can without the average ear spotting it."

Examples of Yip's attention to craft appear in "Happiness is a Thing Called Joe." Happiness and 'jes. Smile and lilac. Way and makes and angels. Sounds repeat inside each line. "It's difficult to do," said Yip, "but it makes the song live, makes it easy to remember, and if the ideas are good, the whole thing begins to sparkle and take on four new lives instead of one."

In 1943, the musical *Oklahoma!* by Richard Rogers and Oscar Hammerstein II opened on Broadway. The show featured songs and dancing that tightly connected to the plot and characters. *Oklahoma!* was funny, but it also had serious dramatic themes.

Oklahoma! marked a major step in the development of musicals that connected a show's songs to its story, a direction that started with *Show Boat* in 1927. It was a huge success. Despite this success, *Oklahoma!* was the only musical of its kind on Broadway until Yip's show, *Bloomer Girl* opened 18 months later.

Yip came up with the idea for *Bloomer Girl* as he thought about the history of women's fashion. In the 1850s, Amelia Bloomer, a true historical heroine, worked for women's rights. She felt that women should stop wearing hoop skirts, which could weigh more than 50 pounds, and instead should wear trousers, so that they could move more easily and be more equal to men. She designed women's trousers which eventually came to be called bloomers. Yip took the idea and made it part of his musical. The show was about women's rights, but it was also about equal rights for black people.

Yip had a hand in every part of the production. He wrote the songs with Harold Arlen, he guided the scriptwriters, he helped choose the actors, and he advised the choreographer. He had become someone who was able to "make his musicals more totally an expression of his own personality and point of view . . . he was the motivating force behind each production," as one writer said. With *Bloomer Girl,* Yip continued to add social commentary to a dramatic musical.

Yip, Harold Arlen, and theater friends in 1944.

When it opened in 1944, *Bloomer Girl* was a critical and popular success. At last Yip had fashioned a show that reflected his views throughout. Most of the discussion about the show centered on its songs and characters; people avoided talking about the political messages. Still, the messages were there. Yip had presented his views, dressing them in Broadway costumes, appealing songs, and an engaging story.

At the same time, Yip was active in Hollywood, and raised money for political causes. He produced the election eve radio broadcast for Franklin Delano Roosevelt's presidential campaign. He enlisted Hollywood actors and singers to help, including celebrities like Humphrey Bogart, Judy Garland, Rita Hayworth, Tallulah Bankhead, Danny Kaye, and Gene Kelly.

Yip included three of his own lyrics in the show, including parodies that made fun of Thomas Dewey, Roosevelt's opponent. To the tune of "The Good Old Summertime," he wrote "In the Good Old Hoover Time" hearkening back to the President people associated with the Depression. The song was introduced on that radio broadcast by James Cagney who then sang it with Groucho Marx and Keenan Wynn. Its lyrics went:

In that good old Hoover time,

In that good old Hoover time.

Lots of jobs for everyone

Bootleg, booze and crime.

Buddies singing everywhere

Can you spare a dime?

Don't go back with Dewey

To that good old Hoover time.

Another song was "Free and Equal Blues" which had roots in the old song "St. James Infirmary." Yip had written it with a folk-style composer named Earl Robinson, who years earlier had written the music for the union anthem "Joe Hill" and other directly politically oriented songs.

At that time in the Army, a white soldier who needed a blood transfusion could demand that the blood come from a white person. The plasma supply was segregated. Yip took this absurd regulation as a starting point for the song.

I went down to that St. James Infirmary, and I saw some plasma there,

I ups and asks the doctor man, "Say was the donor dark or fair?"

The doctor laughed a great big laugh, and he puffed it right in my face,

He said, "A molecule is a molecule, son, and the damn thing has no race."

And that was news, yes that was news,

That was very, very, very special news.

'Cause ever since that day we've had those free and equal blues.

Roosevelt himself spoke during the broadcast, and the next day he was overwhelmingly elected President for his fourth term.

The following spring in 1945, Yip oversaw another broadcast. It was called Unity Fair and it celebrated the conference that established the United Nations. He provided the songs, wrote some of the script, and included a new song he had written with Earl Robinson called "The Same Boat, Brother." The song promoted a view of the unity of the human race.

The Lord looked down from his holy place.

Said Lordy me, what a sea of space.

What a spot to launch the human race.

So he built him a boat for a mixed-up crew,

With eyes of Black and Brown and Blue.

So that's how come that you and I

Got just one world and just one sky.

We're in the same boat, brother,

We're in the same boat, brother,

And if you shake one end,

You gonna rock the other

It's the same boat, brother.

Yip had moved beyond concealing his views inside clever Broadway tunes. These songs with Earl Robinson were very direct. No one would mistake his political perspective after hearing such lyrics.

The broadcast reached millions of people, but Yip would not be able to present his views on network broadcasting again for many years. The political climate changed after World War II. It became more restrictive. Yip had changed too. The importance of speaking to political issues had intensified in him. He stopped working with Harold Arlen, who felt that Yip had lost sight of the entertainment in songs in favor of social commentary.

Yip had an idea for a new show. He wanted to take what he had learned about creating and directing musicals, and use the lessons in a show that would address racism and political hypocrisy even more directly than *Bloomer Girl*. Yip wanted to reach further, and in doing so, he created what many critics would call his masterpiece, *Finian's Rainbow*.

CHAPTER 13

Look to the Rainbow

In the 1940s, racism was rampant in the United States. Black people faced segregation in housing, education, and public transportation. They were discriminated against in the voting booth, and they were often victims of racist violence.

Yip was outraged at the inequality and by elected officials who spouted prejudice and bigotry in their campaigns and legislative work. Yip was also angry at the injustice of the economic system. He remembered his upbringing in poverty and his family's suffering, and he wanted to address these issues in a musical play. *Finian's Rainbow* was the result.

For the first time in Broadway's history, black and white performers danced together, which alone made a significant point about racism. Yip had to fight to make this possible. The lyrics to the show amplified the theme, addressing prejudice and inequality.

Years later, Yip talked about the feelings that led to the show. "Here's a show that was written in 1946. There had been no such song as 'We Shall Overcome.' There was no Martin Luther King. There was just a downright lack of civil rights for a minority of people whose skins were black . . . It's so idiotic . . . nothing seemed to help . . . We thought of one way—how could we prick the bubble of this idiocy? . . . I used a dramatic form that will help us laugh this prejudice out of existence—the musical play."

As usual, Yip wrote the lyrics for the show. Burton Lane wrote the music. Yip co-wrote the script. *Finian's Rainbow* revolves around a man who believes he can grow gold, a leprechaun who pursues him, and a bigoted white senator who is temporarily turned into a black man. Although the gold is gone at the end of the show, the rainbow remains as a symbol of cooperation and goodwill. *Finian's Rainbow* was about serious topics, but it also had a mixture of fantasy, good humor, and memorable songs.

Burton remembered working with Yip. "Yip would get very excited when he heard a tune. He'd bounce all over the room and he'd write. He was already clicking with lyrics." But Yip wasn't always easy to work with. He had strong ideas and could be demanding and harsh toward actors and crew members. One actor said that Yip was a great writer, but not a very good director.

Yip's song "When the Idle Poor Become the Idle Rich" uses humor to make a point about how we see rich and poor people.

When the idle poor become the idle rich

You'll never know just who is who or which is which...

When a rich man doesn't want to work

He's a bon vivant

Yes, he's a bon vivant

But when a poor man doesn't want to work

He's a loafer, he's a lounger

He's a lazy good for nothing

He's a jerk.

For the show, Burton Lane created music in different styles, from classic jazz to blues to Irish folk melodies. "How Are Things in Glocca Morra?" "Old Devil Moon" and "Look to the Rainbow" were hits in the show. Other songs included "When the Idle Rich Become the Idle Poor" and "Necessity."

Yip's lyrics for "Look to the Rainbow" express feelings about dreams and love that fit with his earlier songs. In the song, the singer heads out into the world in search of a dream but only finds it when he returns home and finds happiness in his true love's eyes. In effect, the song says, "There's no place like home."

On the day I was born

Said my father, said he

I've an elegant legacy, waiting for ye

Tis a rhyme for your lips

And a song for your heart

To sing it whenever

The world falls apart

Look, look, look to the rainbow

Follow it over the hill and the stream.

Look, look, look to the rainbow

Follow the fellow who follows a dream.

So I bundled me heart

And I roamed the world free

To the east with the lark

To the west with the sea

And I searched all the earth

And I scanned all the skies

But I found it at last

In my own true love's eyes.

As always, Yip faced the problem of how to write a love song that was fresh and original. In "Old Devil Moon" he writes about the enchantment of love. "There's a little bit of witchcraft in every love," Yip once said.

I look at you and suddenly
Something in your eyes I see
Soon begins bewitching me
It's that old devil moon
That you stole from the skies
It's that old devil moon
In your eyes.

You and your glance
Make this romance
Too hot to handle
Stars in the night
Blazing their light
Can't hold a candle
To your razzle dazzle.

You've got me flying high and wide
On a magic carpet ride
Full of butterflies inside
Wanna cry, wanna croon
Wanna laugh like a loon
It's that old devil moon
In your eyes

Just when I think I'm
Free as a dove
Old devil moon
Deep in your eyes
Blinds me with love.

Yip often liked to use single-word concepts as titles. His song "Necessity" illustrates how Yip liked to contrast one idea against another. In this case, he shows the conflict between doing what you want to and doing what you have to.

What is the curse that makes the universe so all bewild'rin'?

What is the hoax that just provokes the folks they call God's children?

What is the jinx that gives a body and his brother and everyone around

The runaround?

Necessity, Necessity,

That most unnecessary thing, Necessity.

What throws a monkey wrench in

A fella's good intention?

That nasty old invention—Necessity.

My feet wanna' dance in the sun,

My head wants to rest in the shade,

The Lord says, "Go out and have fun,"

But the landlord says, "Your rent ain't paid!"

Necessity, it's plain to see

What a lovely old world this silly old world could be.

But man it's all in a mess, 'cause of Necessity.

Necessity, Necessity,

There oughta' be a law against Necessity.

I'd love to play some tennis,

Or take a trip to Venice.

But sister here's the menace—Necessity.

Oh Satan's the father of sin,

Cupid's the father of love,

Oh, Hell is the father of gin,

But no one knows the father of

Necessity,

That's the maximum that a minimum thing could be,

There's nothing lower than less unless it's Necessity.

Audiences loved *Finian's Rainbow*. It ran for nearly two years. "How Are Things in Glocca Morra?" became a hit for Frank Sinatra. The show received great reviews, too. One reviewer said, "It puts the American musical stage several steps forward for the imagination with which it is written and for the stunning virtuosity of the performance."

Yip talked about his approach to politics in shows. "I've always been aware of the idiocy of the whole establishment and the system. That's what titillated me into using satire. I've always thought that the way to educate, to teach, the way to live without being miserable, even though you're surrounded by misery, was to laugh at the things that made you miserable. For me, satire has become a weapon." He wrote a line for Finian to say. "The situation is hopeless . . . but it's not serious." That line reflects Yip's own view of the world. Even in the most desperate situation, humor is essential.

The political points *Finian's Rainbow* made about racism and capitalism were easy to see if you were looking. However, the story was so engaging and the songs were so entertaining that audiences responded positively, no matter what their own beliefs were.

One critic later wrote, "*Finian's Rainbow* was extraordinarily political, [but] the audience had no idea of that. It was a socialist tract that made its point at a time when the entire country was in fear [of socialism.] If you ever want to reach people with a political tract, go study *Finian's Rainbow*."

Burton Lane and Yip.

CHAPTER 14

Blacklist

World War II ended in 1945, soon after the United States dropped two atomic bombs on Japan. The Allied forces, which included England, Russia, and the United States defeated Germany, Italy, and Japan. Although they had been allies, Russia and the United States soon became enemies. Beginning in 1947 the two sides became hostile to each other, though they never fought directly. The fear and tension between Russia and the U.S. and its allies became known as the Cold War.

Their economic philosophies were in conflict. The capitalistic United States believed that individual freedom and business pursuits were the purpose of society. Communist Russia believed that citizens needed to work together for the common good, and that government's role was to supervise this collective approach.

Their mistrust was not just about philosophy. They had disagreed about how Europe should be divided up after the war. Russia and the United States each believed that the other nation intended to dominate the world. By 1952 the United States had created a more powerful version of the atomic bomb, called the hydrogen bomb. Russian spies stole American secrets that allowed Russia to make and detonate its own hydrogen bomb one year later. The tension between the two nations kept rising.

Many people in America were afraid that the Communists intended to take over the United States. There was deep suspicion of anyone who might be "red," as communists were referred to because of the color of the Communist International flag.

In 1947, the House Un-American Activities Committee held hearings on suspected Communist influence in Hollywood. The mere accusation of being a Communist was enough to destroy a career. Many people's lives were ruined by charges that were usually false. HUAC, as it was called, and Joseph McCarthy, a senator from Wisconsin who propelled suspicions, created a climate in which anyone suspected of having Communist tendencies was blacklisted.

A blacklist is a list of people who are denied services, privileges, or work for reasons that aren't legitimate. In this case, it applied to people who may have had certain political beliefs. The Committee wanted to discover who had been a Communist, but they also created an atmosphere of blame, mistrust, and suspicion by bullying witnesses to turn in their friends and colleagues.

Blacklisting was particularly powerful in Hollywood. Studios denied many artists, writers, and actors the chance to work in movies for fear of being attacked by politicians in Washington. The studios also began to make movies that were blatantly patriotic to deflect criticism.

In 1950, Yip was working on a musical version of *Huckleberry Finn* when MGM's lawyer called him in. Yip remembered that meeting. The lawyer asked Yip, "'Look here, what are your politics?' and all that nonsense and I said I had never joined the Communist party. I had just been one of those vociferous guys who was fighting injustice."

Yip was paid and let go from the movie. Yip tried to clear his name, writing to MGM, saying, "As a firm, almost fanatical believer in democracy, as a proud American, and as the writer of the lyric of the song 'God's Country,' I am outraged by the suggestion that somehow I am connected, believe in, or am sympathetic with Communist or totalitarian philosophy . . . To think that I would belong to any organization which has for its purpose the violent overthrown of our form of government, its constitution, or its institutions, is palpably absurd."

Although Yip protested that he had never been a Communist, merely being associated with organizations that had included Communists was enough. He was blacklisted from working in Hollywood, or on radio, or TV, and he did not work in those places for 12 years.

Yip was not alone. Many other actors, actresses, composers, and writers were also accused. The list included: Orson Welles, director and actor, Dorothy Parker, writer, Aaron Copland, composer, Leonard Bernstein, composer and conductor, Burl Ives, folk singer and actor, Pete Seeger, folksinger, Langston Hughes, writer, and Zero Mostel, actor.

Some collaborated with the committee, and others refused. Jay Gorney, the composer who had written the music for "Brother Can You Spare a Dime" was carried out of the Senate chamber because he began to sing a song he'd written called "First Amendment." Earl Robinson, another of Yip's partners, took what he called "the diminished fifth." He admitted his membership in the Communist party, but refused to name others who were also members. Some witnesses who refused to cooperate went to jail.

Yip's maintained his innocence. He was told that if he would write an article for the American Legion magazine admitting that he was a Communist and acknowledging that he was wrong, he could work in Hollywood again. He refused with humor, saying that he was a first class writer and he wouldn't write for a third class publication.

Yip later wrote a short verse about being accused unfairly, and about those who did choose to name names in an attempt to clear their own.

For the Birds

The Eagle—fierce omnivorous vulture—

Noble emblem of our culture,

Has been reduced to just a smidgen;

Who cooked his goose? The cool stool pigeon.

Yip said that being blacklisted was "very traumatic, but it didn't floor me." Royalties from his many songs provided an income of over 150,000 dollars a year for him to live on. He was able to lend money to other artists who were blacklisted and who didn't have money. Fortunately, the blacklist did not extend to Broadway.

Yip working with a tape recorder. 1950's

In 1951, Yip created a Broadway show called *Flahooley*. It was about a toy doll factory, and the show included puppets and dolls, as well as dancing and songs. The show addressed political issues like atomic energy and the United States economic system. Its staging was unique on Broadway, but its plot wasn't compelling enough, and the score didn't have any major hits. When it closed after only 48 performances, losing money, it was Yip's first commercial failure on Broadway since 1932.

Yip kept trying to work in Hollywood. He was almost cleared to work on the movie *A Star is Born* with Judy Garland, but in the end the movie studio wouldn't take a chance on him. Sometimes he came close. "We did *The Wizard of Oz* and then they never used us for another fantasy film . . . Sam Goldwyn did hire me to do *Hans Christian Anderson* but when I was on my way to the airport, they telephoned me and told me not to come."

"I lost one picture after another," said Yip. "It was not only frightening, but it just took all your dignity away and you realized what it is to live in a police state and understand the fear that people in such countries have of not knowing what's going to happen next . . . It keeps hitting you. Some of the fellows, my friends, did commit suicide . . . all around there was heartbreak and misery." Yip wasn't even allowed to have a passport for three years.

In 1956, Yip, Fred Saidy, and Harold Arlen had created a show called *Pigeon Island*. It was going to feature a rising young star named Harry Belafonte. The show used calypso and Caribbean style music as it contrasted America's materialistic lifestyle with an imaginary primitive island. The show's name was eventually changed to *Jamaica*.

Jamaica included "Napoleon" which looks at how time diminishes everyone, even famous people. "Leave De Atom Alone," anticipates later protest songs about nuclear energy. Yip's use of "de" instead of "the" parodied commercial Calypso-style music.

Leave de atom alone

Leave de atom alone.

Don't get smart alecksy

With de galaxy.

Leave de atom alone.

If you like Paris in the Springtime

London in de Fall

Manhattan in de Summer

With music on de mall.

Stop fooling with de fallout

Above de cosmic ball

Or you will soon be fissionable material.

It also included one of Yip's trademark philosophy songs "For Every Fish."

Man he eat the barracuda. Barracuda eat the bass.

Bass eat the little flounder, cause the flounder's lower class.

Little flounder eat the sardine. It's nature's plan.

Little sardine eat the worm. Worm eat the man.

For every fish there's a bigger fish...

When Harry Belafonte became sick, the producers enlisted a popular young singer named Lena Horne. The producers changed much of the script to showcase Lena's singing. People came to hear Lena Horne, but the story had been weakened, losing the original power of Yip's intentions. Although the show ran for over 500 performances, Yip didn't like it. He knew that the message had been lost. "I did not come in for the opening of *Jamaica*," he said. "I did not feel spiritually attached to it . . . However . . . it is off to a smash hit . . . I will take the cash and let the credit go." Still, the show had a completely African-American cast, which was a daring step for Broadway.

In 1962, Yip returned to Hollywood to work with Harold Arlen on a score for a cartoon movie called *Gay Purr-ee*, which featured the singing of Judy Garland and Robert Goulet. The blacklist was over, but the days of the Hollywood musical Yip had helped to create were passing, too. His collaborators were aging, and musical styles were changing. Yip didn't think that the new generation of composers had as much talent as the men he had worked with before. Yip wanted to keep working, but it appeared that time was passing him by.

Yip and Fred Saidy.

CHAPTER 15

The Sixties

In 1961 Yip brought another show to Broadway, called *The Happiest Girl in the World*. Yip adapted an ancient Greek play called *Lysistrata* for the story, which had an anti-war theme. He hired Jay Gorney to sift through the music of a composer named Jacques Offenbach, who had died 80 years earlier. Jay Gorney assembled a score from melodies found in Offenbach's operas, and Yip wrote the lyrics to what Jay had put together. It was an unusual type of collaboration. However, *The Happiest Girl in the World* ran for only 97 performances.

Yip continued to write songs. He also wrote poems and light verse, many of which commented on what he saw happening in the world. He wrote a poem about a writer who had been censored by the Russian leader Nikita Khrushchev.

Yevtushenko

"I'm not afraid of atom bombs"

said Khrushchev, "And they know it;

I'm not afraid of anything,

Except, perhaps, a poet."

He addressed religion, too.

Where Bishop Patrick crossed the street

An X now marks the spot.

The light of God was with him

But the traffic light was not.

In 1963, Yip and Harold Arlen wrote a beautiful and frightening song inspired by Rachel Carson's book, "Silent Spring", which was a milestone in the beginning of the environmental movement, documenting the deadly effect of pesticides. Yip and Harold's song captures images of ecological destruction.

The Silent Spring

Not a leaf is heard to murmur,

Not a bird is there to sing

And bewild'ring eyes

Scan the fearful skies

Asking why this strange and silent Spring?

Yip goes on to call for action to save the earth, and frames it with the power of music.

Silent men, take heart, take wing.

Sing away this silent spring.

In the 1960s protest music became popular. Folk singers and rock bands wrote and performed songs that commented directly on social issues and called for action to change the world. Songs about civil rights and the Vietnam War flooded the airwaves and record stores.

Yip appreciated their political views, but he felt that the writers lacked musical and lyrical sophistication. He wanted songwriters to pay careful attention to rhyme, rhythm, and subtlety of meaning. He also expected songs to have memorable and carefully developed music. Songwriters who created a song in the afternoon and then rushed to perform it that night weren't using the craft of deliberate and thoughtful writing that Yip and others of his generation had spent years cultivating. These new songs often lacked humor or intricate language, which could make them more appealing to those who might not share the same political viewpoint. In

1976 Andrew Tully summarized Yip's opinion in a column for the San Francisco Chronicle. "He welcomes today's revolution. He just wishes they could write music."

Yip wrote a poem about his feelings.

Music on the Rocks

Hail the songs, the latest rages

Dripping from guitar and pen,

All are destined for the ages—

Like I mean, from five to ten.

He went on to comment directly. "The new songs are antigrammatical and antipoetical. They're tasteless, violent, and unmelodic." Yip would probably not have been a fan of most rap music, although he might have appreciated the rhyming and word play rap artists improvised. There were many songwriters, like Bob Dylan, Roger Miller and the Beatles, whose lyrics were well crafted, but Yip was writing about most of the popular songs he heard.

Yip did write a folk type song with Earl Robinson called "Hurry Sundown," which was a minor hit for Peter, Paul, and Mary.

In 1965, Yip published a collection of poems called "Rhymes for the Irreverent." Eleven years later he published another, called "At This Point in Rhyme." Many years later the two books were combined into one volume called simply "Rhymes for the Irreverent."

In 1968, Warner Brothers made a movie version of *Finian's Rainbow*. Francis Ford Coppola, who went on to make *The Godfather* films, directed the movie. It starred Fred Astaire, but Yip thought it was a disaster, completely losing the intention of his original musical. The film still survives, available in DVD, because of its great songs.

Through the 1960s and 70s, Yip kept working with various composers. He hoped to put together a revue of his songs for Broadway, but it never got off the ground.

In 1970, he helped start a concert and lecture series called "Lyrics and Lyricists" at New York's 92nd Street Y. The program was an opportunity for writers to perform and discuss their lyrics. Yip believed that musical theater was one of America's great artistic contributions to the world, and yet he and other writers of his generation were concerned that the skills and values of theater writing were being lost. The 92nd Street Y program was one way to communicate and discuss the qualities of the art form, and it has been so successful that the series continues to this day.

In 1980 Yip helped to found a graduate program at NYU in Musical Theater Writing. Yip wanted young writers to have the opportunity to learn the craft of writing for the musical theatre. Learning the skill of collaborating with other writers was central to its mission. Yip's future daughter-in-law became this unique program's founding chair.

He was influential and helpful to other writers as well. Stephen Sondheim remembers performing for a gathering at Yip's apartment, and being encouraged in his work. In his book "Finishing the Hat," Sondheim cites Yip's influence. "Harburg, Porter and Berlin were the most brilliant technicians of the Golden Age. Harburg was the maverick, pointedly socio-political and heavily whimsical . . . Harburg was at his best when the subject matter suited his fanciful style . . . One of my favorite lines is from *'Bloomer Girls'*—'Even the rabbits inhibit their habits on Sunday in Cicero Falls.'"

In 1972, Yip was inducted into the Songwriters Hall of Fame. He was also recognized as a survivor of the McCarthy era blacklisting as the country realized that McCarthyism was wrong. Pete Seeger famously said, "One of the things I'm most proud of about my country is the fact that we did lick McCarthyism back in the fifties." Yip would have agreed and in this poem he reflects on history..

Lives of great men all remind us greatness takes no easy way,

All the heroes of tomorrow are the heretics of today.

Socrates and Galileo, John Brown,Thoreau, Christ and Debs

Heard the night cry "Down with traitors!" And the dawn shout "Up the rebs!"

Nothing ever seems to bust them—Gallows, crosses, prison bars;

Tho'we try to readjust them, there they are among the stars.

Lives of great men all remind us we can write our names on high

And departing leave behind us thumbprints in the FBI.

Yip never stopped writing and working. He was interviewed on television several times, including an interview on *60 Minutes* in 1978. In 1981, he was driving to a meeting about writing lyrics for a new movie based on the book "Treasure Island." He suffered a heart attack and died instantly. He was 84 years old.

Several years earlier, in true Yip Harburg style, he'd written a poem about his own death.

I've whittled my wit

And whipped my rhymes

For a small obit

In the New York Times.

Facing death was hopeless, but not serious.

Yip around the time of his appearance on 60 minutes. 1970s

CHAPTER 16

Legacy

Yip Harburg's songs are rooted in a particular time—the birth and flowering of the Broadway musical. He was a member of an elite group of writers, including Oscar Hammerstein, Cole Porter, and Ira Gershwin, who transformed the nature of Broadway theater. His lyrics are more sophisticated than the Tin Pan Alley songs that came before him, or the rock and pop songs that followed him in the 60s and 70s. His training in classical forms of poetry and his careful attention to rhyme, meter, sound, and progression of meaning make him a closer relative to Shakespeare than to the Rolling Stones.

The composers with whom he collaborated also came from a classical background, although blues and folk styles influenced them all. Their songs were in the popular vein, but their emphasis on developing melodies and intricate harmonies created music that was much more refined and complicated than most popular music today.

Although Yip's songs are reflections of that particular time, many of them live on still, loved, appreciated, and performed around the world.

"Over the Rainbow" has been recorded by hundreds of artists, including Eric Clapton, Billy Ray Cyrus, Celine Dion, Barbara Streisand, Ray Charles, and Frank Sinatra. In 1993, Israel Kamakawiwo'ole recorded a medley of "Over the Rainbow/What a Wonderful World" that reached #12 on the Billboard charts, and sold millions of copies. Eva Cassidy's 1996 version is particularly wonderful, as the song takes on a modern, yet timeless quality.

Noted folk singer Pete Seeger sang "Over the Rainbow" in his concerts for years. He would encourage the audience to sing along with him. "I sing it in the key of A. I line out the melody like a hymn, all the way through. If it's not too fast I can get the words in between, feeding the lyrics to the audience. I tell the crowd there are two more lines. Somewhere up there I can hear Yip saying, 'Pete, you can mess with your folk songs but leave mine alone.' I do it anyway. The lyrics ask, 'Why oh why can't I?' You know why you can't? Because you are only asking for yourself. So I add two words—why can't *you* and I? Then we hold those last notes, making a perfect triad."

Yip would have disagreed with Pete Seeger's change. Yip's strength as a lyricist who was concerned with political or social issues is in his ability to help the listener see things through one person's eyes, in a personal way. Pete Seeger's lyric change shows where two lyrical traditions collide—the careful craftsman, who chooses each word precisely, and the folk singer, who changes songs as needed to fit a situation.

Pete Seeger also wrote a melody for one of Yip's poems, called "The Odds on Favorite." Pete first sang it in the newly named Yip Harburg Auditorium at P.S. 19 on New York's Lower East Side, near where Yip had grown up. The renovation of that school was paid for with royalties from Yip's songs.

"Brother, Can You Spare a Dime?" has been sung by hundreds of artists. Peter, Paul and Mary, Tiny Tim, Judy Collins, and Tom Waits are a few of the singers who have recorded it. It's an anthem that surfaces whenever people face hard times. In 1984 during a large miners' strike in England, "Brother Can You Spare a Dime?" was a central song in the struggle. During the global economic collapse of 2008, the song took on new relevance as millions of people lost their jobs and their homes.

Other songs, like "April in Paris" and "Old Devil Moon" have become jazz standards for singers and instrumentalists. "It's Only a Paper Moon" became the title of a popular 1973 movie of the same name. "Lydia the Tattooed Lady" continues to be a comic gem for singers and choirs.

In the late 1970s some of Yip's family created the Yip Harburg Foundation. The Foundation dedicates money from Yip's song royalties to peace and social justice issues. Yip's son Ernie remembers presenting the documents for the Foundation to Yip.

"Yip was visibly touched, and I wound up saying, 'And so, Yip, we're giving you a gift of an elegant legacy,' which were words from one of his lyrics in *Finian's Rainbow*. (I've an elegant legacy waitin' for ye.) In his eyes I saw simultaneously appear a tear and a twinkle. And this is absolute Yip. No matter what it was, he had a humorous take on it. He leaned back in his chair and said, 'Oh, come now, you're pulling my legacy.'"

In 1996, the room at the Tompkins Square Library where Yip had spent so many hours as a child was formally named the Yip Harburg Reading Room in his honor. Yip had nurtured his early love of words there, while trying to stay warm in the winter.

In April of 2005, the U.S. Post Office honored him by issuing a first class stamp with the words "Somewhere over the rainbow, skies are blue" and a rainbow rising behind a photo of Yip.

In the end, we remember Yip most for "Over the Rainbow." The power of dreams and the courage it takes to make them come true are reoccurring themes throughout Yip's lyrics. Yip himself dared to dream about making a life as a writer and about working to improve society. His dream led him toward the theater, lyrics, songs, and into the hearts of millions around the world with dreams of their own.

Yip said, "A rainbow is a symbolic link between man and the heaven of imagination . . . I've laid great store in man's imaginative ability, on man's ability to be bigger than death, bigger than life in his imagination. Man's imagination is what takes him out of his misery."

"Look to the Rainbow," says Yip. "Dare to Dream." "And remember the power of a song."

CHAPTER 17

Lessons from a Master

Yip Harburg was passionate about the art and craft of lyric writing. He wanted great lyrics from himself, and he was generous in his desire for everyone's lyrics to be the best they could be. He helped his colleagues and friends, he mentored young writers, he lectured on the art form, and he helped create a college program to teach aspiring lyricists.

We can draw a few conclusions or ideas from Yip's life and songs. Yip often discussed his views of lyric writing as he grew older. These are not just Yip's ideas; most lyricists would agree with the majority of these principles.

These are rules to keep in mind when writing songs. Not all of Yip's songs follow all of these rules every time; there are plenty of exceptions. Nevertheless, in general, Yip kept these principles in mind as he crafted his lyrics.

1. Words in songs are important. They matter. They're not there just to keep the beat going or to fill out the melody. What they mean and how they say it make a difference. Words in songs are communicating ideas with the advantage of music, which adds greater feeling.

2. A lyricist should always try to say things in a new way. The listener likes to be surprised. Clichés are easy but boring.

3. Rhymes in a song are best if they are unusual. "You" and "do" has been used millions of times in songs. "With the thoughts I'd be thinkin' I could be another Lincoln," is funny and fresh. Even when rhymes are

unusual, they also have to sound natural, not forced. Internal rhyme and similar sounds (assonance) also help the listener connect to the words.

4. If a song has a twist at the end, it is more effective, especially if the song is meant to be funny or clever. Listeners stay more engaged in the song if there is an unexpected gift at the end.

5. A song should start with a feeling. Music establishes an emotion that the words build on.

6. It's best if the meter of a line is perfect. A singer shouldn't have to squeeze in extra syllables or hold out a word to make the words fit the music. The length of the line and the melody should fit like a comfortable and favorite shoe.

7. Unusual words catch the listener's attention.

8. If a song is for a show, it should connect to the story and the characters. It must add something essential, so that if you took it out, the audience would feel like something was missing.

9. Writing lyrics, like any writing, is hard work. Yip was a perfectionist, and he wasn't afraid to spend hours coming up with just the right word. He also wasn't afraid to throw out an idea he'd worked on for a long time if a better idea came along.

10. Lyric writing is cooperative and collaborative. You need to work with the composer. You can also get good ideas and helpful criticism from other writers. Getting help will improve your writing.

11. Writing songs is joyful. Yip loved his work and was good at it because he loved it. His good humor and his pleasure in putting words together created the masterpieces that we still know and sing today.

Author's note

We passed the word around, whispering in class and talking on the playground or on the way home from school.

"The Wizard is on." "Are you going to watch the Wizard?" "Sunday night, it's on."

When Sunday night arrived, my family settled in to watch the annual showing of *The Wizard of Oz*. Millions of other families did the same. In the days before cable, VCRS, DVDs and streaming internet connections, the only chance to watch the movie came at its once a year broadcast.

When Dorothy leaned against a fence and sang the first words, "Somewhere over the Rainbow," millions of viewers sighed and leaned back into their seats, ready once again to enter the magical world of Oz. The song was a signal to all of us that the wonderful journey was about to begin.

Lyricists are often unknown. They are not famous, like actors or performers. Their names don't grace the covers of books. We sing the words to their songs, but we usually don't know who wrote them.

Although almost no one knows Yip Harburg by name, everyone knows his songs. When I heard a radio interview with Yip's son Ernie Harburg, I was fascinated with Yip's life and his place in the history of musical theater and film. The more I learned, the more interested I became. I became convinced that Yip Harburg was one of America's greatest lyricists, and that his songs will continue to reach an audience for many years to come.

As a songwriter, I recognize the value of Yip's contribution to the art form. Although Yip may not be a household name, songwriters everywhere respect and revere him and count him as an influence. As I wrote about Yip's life, I began to reflect on my own music, and I have to say that I learned something about lyric writing at every step of his story.

I'm grateful to the Yip Harburg Foundation, and in particular Deena and Ernie Harburg and Nick Markovich. Ernie is Yip's son, and he has two fine books that explore Yip's life and legacy in much greater depth than this one. The Foundation provided financial support for the development of this manuscript, which was a great gift.

I'm particularly grateful to Peter Berryman, an extraordinary lyricist in his own right. Over the course of many conversations he helped me to think about what was essential in this story, in particular about lyric writing.

My appreciation extends to others who read drafts of the book: Barbara Chusid, Daniel Sklar, Dave Kinnoin, and Christine Hayes. My ongoing critique group of Jacqueline Houtman, Darcy Miller, and Roxanne Cornell, had helpful suggestions as well.

Special thanks to my lovely daughters Cerisa and Calli for watching the *Wizard of Oz* over and over when they were young. Cerisa was a fine editor and overseer of this manuscript, and her contributions have improved the text. And to my wife Heather for all of her support and enthusiasm for music, in life, and in education.

Song Credits

Big Valley Press has attempted to contact all parties involved with acquiring the copyright for Yip Harburg's songs. If we have failed to mention any party, or neglected to include correct information, please contact us and we will be happy to correct any mistakes.

"April in Paris" by E.Y. "Yip" Harburg and Vernon Duke
Published by Hal Leonard Corp.
Copyright © (1932)
All Rights Reserved

"Brother, Can You Spare a Dime?" by E.Y. "Yip" Harburg and Jay Gorney
Published by Gorney Music (ASCAP)
Gorney Music Administered by Next Decade Entertainment, Inc.
Copyright © (1932)
All Rights Reserved

"Fun to be Fooled" Music by Harold Arlen, Lyrics by E.Y. "Yip" Harburg
Published by SA Music, LLC and Glocca Morra Music/ASCAP
Copyright © (1934)
Used by permission

"Happiness is a Thing Called Joe" Music by Harold Arlen, Lyrics by E.Y. "Yip" Harburg
Published by SA Music, LLC and Glocca Morra Music/ASCAP
Copyright © (1943)
Used by permission

"It's Only a Paper Moon" by E.Y. "Yip" Harburg, Harold Arlen and Billy Rose
Published by Hal Leonard Corp.
Copyright © (1932)
All Rights Reserved

"Last Night When We Were Young" Music by Harold Arlen, Lyrics by E.Y. "Yip" Harburg
Published by SA Music, LLC and Glocca Morra Music/ASCAP
Copyright © (1935)
Used by permission

"Leave De Atom Alone" Music by Harold Arlen, Lyrics by E.Y. "Yip" Harburg
Copyright © (1957)
Used by permission

"Look to the Rainbow" Music by Burton Lane, Lyrics by E.Y. "Yip" Harburg
Copyright © (1947)
Used by permission

"Lydia, the Tattooed Lady" Music by Harold Arlen, Lyrics by E.Y. "Yip" Harburg
Published by SA Music, LLC and Glocca Morra Music/ASCAP
Copyright © (1939)
Used by permission

"Necessity" Music by Burton Lane, Lyrics by E.Y. "Yip" Harburg
Copyright © (1947)
Used by permission

"Old Devil Moon" Music by Burton Lane, Lyrics by E.Y. "Yip" Harburg
Copyright © (1947)
Used by permission

"That's Life" by E.Y. "Yip" Harburg and Vernon Duke
Published by Hal Leonard Corp.
Copyright © (1932)
All Rights Reserved

"The Same Boat, Brother" by E.Y. "Yip" Harburg and Earl Robinson
Published by Hal Leonard Corp.
Copyright © (1945)
All Rights Reserved

"The Silent Spring" Music by Harold Arlen, Lyrics by E.Y. "Yip" Harburg
Copyright © (1963)
Used by permission

"When the Idle Poor Become the Idle Rich" Music by Burton Lane, Lyrics by E.Y. "Yip" Harburg
Copyright © (1947)
Used by permission

Bibliography

Alonso, Harriet Hyman. *Yip Harburg: Legendary Lyricist and Human Rights Activist (Music/Interview)*. Wesleyan, 2012

Harburg, Ernie and Harold Meyerson. *Who Put the Rainbow in The Wizard of Oz?: Yip Harburg, Lyricist*. University of Michigan Press, 1995

Harburg, Yip. *The Yip Harburg Songbook*. Hal Leonard, 2009

Harburg, Yip. *Rhymes for the Irreverent*. Freedom From Religion Foundation, 2006

Stotts, Stuart. *We Shall Overcome: A Song That Changed the World*. New York: Clarion, 2010

Internet Resources

Yip Harburg talking about Rainbows. http://www.youtube.com/watch?v=eNiXnzh3abk

Yip Harburg Foundation. www.yipharburg.com

Introductory Article about Yip. https://thegreenwichvillageliteraryreview.wordpress.com/2015/06/16/yip-harburg-a-lyrical-activist-against-social-injustice-by-leigh-donaldson-with-ernie-harburg/

About the Author

Stuart Stotts is a songwriter, author, and educational consultant who lives in Deforest, Wi. He travels throughout the United States performing and presenting at conferences and educational training events. Stuart was ably assisted in the development of this manuscript by his daughter Cerisa Obern, a multi-talented linguist and world traveller. Stuart's other books include *Father Groppi: Civil Rights Leader*, *Books in a Box: Lutie Stearns and the Traveling Libraries of Wisconsin*, and *We Shall Overcome: A Song That Changed the World*. Stuart is married to Heather Terrill Stotts. You can find out more about him at his website, www.StuartStotts.com

Foreword by . . .

Peter Berryman is the lyricist in the duo Peter and Lou Berryman. Their songs have delighted audiences for nearly fifty years with their audacious wit, their singeable melodies, and their one of a kind lyrics. More information at www.louandpeter.com

www.ingramcontent.com/pod-product-compliance
Lightning Source LLC
Chambersburg PA
CBHW081945070426
42450CB00016BA/3427